Supporting Children with Learning Difficulties

Also available in the Supporting Children Series

Supporting Deaf Children and Young People, Derek Brinkley

Supporting Children with ADHD 2nd Edition, Kate Spohrer

Supporting Children with Dyslexia 2nd Edition, Garry Squires and Sally McKeown

Also Available from Continuum

The Dyscalculia Assessment, Jane Emerson and Patricia Babtie

Dyslexia 3rd Edition, Gavin Reid

Supporting Children with Learning Difficulties

Holistic Solutions for Severe, Profound and Multiple Disabilities

CHRISTINE TURNER

B L O O M S B U R Y
LONDON · NEW DELHI · NEW YORK · SYDNEY

Published 2012 by Continuum
an imprint of Bloomsbury Publishing Plc
50 Bedford Square, London W1B 3DP

www.bloomsbury.com

ISBN: 978-1-4411-2177-6 (paperback)

© Christine Turner 2011

First published 2011 by Continuum International Publishing Group
Reprinted 2012 (twice)

A CIP record for this publication is available from the British Library.

Typeset by Newgen Imaging Systems Pvt Ltd, Chennai, India
Printed and bound in Great Britain

This book is produced using paper that is made from wood grown in managed,
sustainable forests. It is natural, renewable and recyclable. The logging and
manufacturing processes conform to the environmental regulations of the
country of origin.

Contents

Preface

The inspiration for this book came from a friend and colleague at the special school where I worked for many years. She had little experience of children with learning disabilities and expressed concern about the lack of clearly written and easily accessible information covering all aspects of severe, profound and multiple learning disabilities. Feeling sure that the information she sought must already be available, I began to investigate. There were books discussing issues as varied as conditions and syndromes, inclusion, behaviour, communication, curriculum and legislation, all of which were well-written and informative. Some were very prescriptive, telling what to teach and when to teach it while others were full of facts, figures and statistics. Most were aimed either at parents and carers or at those in education, with very few looking at the complete child.

That is where this book differs from most others. It does not dwell on or describe specific conditions or syndromes, since information on these is readily available. Nor does it discuss current legislation, since legislation changes frequently and soon becomes outdated. It does not tell what to teach or when to teach it, as children with learning disabilities may not follow the usual patterns of learning. Instead, it explores the way teachers, parents and carers can optimize learning among individuals with severe, profound or multiple learning disabilities and allows them to understand how the child's disabilities can affect learning and development. By encouraging those reading it to place themselves in the shoes of the learning-disabled child, it also provides a brief, but essential, insight into their world. Use of technical jargon is purposely avoided to allow this book to be easily read and understood by as wide an audience as possible.

From the initial chapters outlining some of the causes of a learning disability and the way the disability affects the whole family, the book aims to paint a picture of the child as a whole. Numerous tips and stories based on real-life situations are included as well as suggestions and techniques to ensure every child is able to make progress and develop confidence in his or her own abilities. Although primarily aimed at children with severe, profound and multiple learning disabilities it may also be adapted, if necessary, to help other children who, for one reason or another, require extra help to learn or consolidate skills in particular areas.

As well as being essential reading for those in education, namely students, teachers and teaching assistants, the book will also be of interest to parents and carers, staff in residential or respite care centres, healthcare staff and anyone else involved in the day to day care of children with severe, profound and multiple learning disabilities. Based on personal experience, it discusses the way learning disabled children actually learn, act and develop rather than the way experts predict they should. It does not profess to cover every aspect of learning disabilities, since that would be impossible in a book of this size. It can be read from cover to cover to provide an excellent, extensive introduction to the learning-disabled child (and this is the best way to read the book if a full understanding of the child is to be achieved). It can also be dipped into as needed or used as a stepping-stone for those who wish to increase their knowledge and skills. For this reason, further reading suggestions and a list of relevant websites are included at the back of the book.

I hope you will enjoy reading this book and that it enables you to teach more effectively, work with greater confidence or live with greater awareness of the children around you. Always remember, though, that every child is different, and that each is an individual in his or her own right. Be prepared to learn from them as they will undoubtedly learn from you.

Acknowledgements

I would like to begin by thanking Carol Bidmead whose original suggestion it was to write this book and who was always available on the end of the phone to encourage me and spur me on. Thanks also to Anthea Crofts, Lucy Gwynn-Jones, Claire Melless, Penny Reid and Teresa Simpson for their comments, and thanks to all those who generously gave their time to check my proof pages. I would also like to thank Rachel Cook for her advice on communication and Bill Fisher for providing the artwork.

Thanks must also go to everyone at the Makaton Charity and to Donna Banzhof, M.Ed., BCBA from Pyramid Educational Consultants, USA, for checking my facts, as well to Tim Swingler from Soundbeam. Finally, I am grateful to Inclusive Technology Ltd, QED and ROMPA for allowing me to include illustrations of their products.

The biggest 'THANK YOU's of all, though, must go to three sets of people without whom none of this would have been possible.

First, thanks to my Mum and Dad who encouraged me to fulfil my childhood ambition and supported me through my years of teacher training. Without them my life may have taken a very different route.

Second, thank you to my husband, Rob, and my three children, Paul, Laura and Michael as well as, more recently, to Delia, Paul's wife. Their support and encouragement have been never-ending, not just while writing this book but also during my time teaching. I could not have completed this book without their help.

Finally, I would like to thank all the children I have had the privilege of teaching over the past twenty-five years. They have made me laugh, made me cry, caused headaches and heartbreak, joy and satisfaction. They have taught me patience and tolerance and have allowed me to join them in celebrating their achievements, no matter how small. They have shown me the importance of the little things in life and have encouraged me never to take things for granted. They have taught me much, for which I will be eternally grateful.

A note on terminology

Over the years, children who have learning disabilities have been given a variety of names and labels to describe their conditions. In the past, they have been referred to as mentally retarded, imbeciles or mentally handicapped, while, more recently, they have been described as having learning disabilities, learning difficulties, learning impairments or special needs. These labels change on a regular basis, and it is often difficult to keep up to date with current terminology. Some of these terms are more descriptive than others, and while some are self explanatory (e.g., learning difficulties), others are less so. The term 'special needs' for example, can cover a wide variety of conditions, including, among others, learning difficulties, sensory impairments, physical disabilities, medical conditions such as epilepsy or severe allergy and even includes those children who are particularly gifted.

The terms 'learning disabilities' and 'learning difficulties' are often used in conversation or written work to mean one and the same thing, and many involved in the education and day-to-day care of children with impaired learning are unable to differentiate between the two. This inevitably leads to confusion over which term to use. Even among professionals, there is no consistency, and while many appear to use 'learning difficulty' regardless of the child's condition, others favour 'learning disability'. Parents often have their own preference and even the media seems confused about which to use.

There is, however, a very distinct difference between these two conditions. To put it simply a learning difficulty suggests the presence of a specific learning problem such as dyslexia, while a learning disability implies a more general intellectual impairment. On the basis of these definitions, as well as personal experience, it could be argued that some with learning disabilities may also have additional learning difficulties.

There remains, however, much ambiguity in the use of these terms, and the distinction between the two appears erratic. Consequently, those who, for one reason or another, do not progress along the normal developmental route as quickly as other children of the same age will be identified in this book as having a 'learning disability'. The exception to this is the term 'profound and multiple learning difficulties', which is a recognised condition in its own right. To aid readability, and purely for this reason, occasionally the terms 'learning impaired' or 'learning disabled' may also be used.

Note

Throughout this book, for the sake of readability, I have used 'he' rather than 'he or she' when referring to a child with learning disabilities, but please do read this as being applicable to both sexes. I have also taken the liberty of using the word 'parent' to refer to anyone who cares for the child, including grandparents, other family members, friends or carers.

Certain details of the stories, including names, have been changed in order to protect the identities of those concerned.

1 | A brief introduction to learning disabilities

Each child brings its own blessing into the world.

–Yiddish proverb

Children with learning disabilities are born into all types of families, irrespective of creed, race or status. They are born into communities all over the world, from towns and cities to remote villages and hillside settlements although, for most, it is only during the last century that they have started to take their rightful place in society.

In the past, the fate of children born with learning disabilities has varied according to local culture and belief. At best, they have been regarded as gifts from God, the so-called 'Holy Innocents', while at worst (and unfortunately more frequently) they have been accused of being the result of an evil or illicit relationship, or a punishment for unacceptable behaviours. Over the course of time, they have been treated with both pity and ridicule, associated with witchcraft, regarded as infectious, left on mountainsides to die, or locked away in asylums. Names to describe them have been less than flattering: imbeciles, retards, lunatics, idiots, degenerates, subhuman, cretins or mental defectives, to name but a few.

Until recent times, a lack of medical care and knowledge often prevented those born with the most severe learning disabilities from living beyond birth or infancy, regardless of society's views at the time. Those with only a mild learning disability may have fared better. Without the need to read, write or perform intellectual tasks, many would have coped well with the labour-intensive farming and manual labour tasks required of a slower, less stressful lifestyle. However, as the ability to think, plan, organize and compete on an intellectual basis has become more valued than the qualities of physical strength and endurance, society has become increasingly aware of children and adults with mild to moderate learning disabilities.

Even today, the exact number of people born with a learning disability remains difficult to assess and the statistics vary according to their source. At the time of writing, the charity Mencap (www.mencap.org.uk, November 2010) estimates that 1.5 million people in the United Kingdom have some form of learning disability. A Department of Health white paper entitled 'Valuing

People – A New Strategy for Learning Disability for the 21st Century' (March 2001) breaks this down further. This study estimates that in England alone there are around 1.2 million people with mild or moderate learning disabilities, approximately 2.5 per cent of the population, while 210,000 have severe or profound learning disabilities. Inevitably there will be some – especially those in the older age group – who, because they are able to cope on a daily basis without any diagnosis or recognition of their learning impairment, are not included in any statistics.

Categorizing learning disabilities

The ability of those with learning disabilities varies according to the extent of their impairment. Generally, they fall into one of four categories and are described as having a mild, moderate, severe or profound learning disability. There are several ways of assessing the level of disability, with some ways being more appropriate than others.

To begin, let us first determine the levels according to traditional methods. Formal intelligence tests, the forerunner of modern day IQ (intelligence quotient) tests, were used as far back as 1905 in France by Alfred Binet to ensure that children with learning disabilities received the most appropriate schooling. Nowadays, however, adults or children of almost any age or ability can be assessed using a variety of different IQ tests. According to these, the average person will have an IQ of 100 while those with an IQ rating of less than 70 will be classed as having a learning disability. Within this, those with an IQ of 50 to 70 will be classified as having a mild learning disability, those with an IQ of 35 to 50 are deemed to have a moderate learning disability, and those with an IQ of 20 to 35 are described as having a severe learning disability. Those with an IQ rating of less than 20 are regarded as having a profound learning disability.

A major problem with these tests, however, lies in the fact that intelligence is not only difficult to define, but also difficult to measure. An ability to perform well in English, maths and other academic studies, for example, may result in a higher IQ score than skills in music or the arts. Cultural differences, environmental factors and language barriers can also affect the final result, as can a child's interest or attitude on the day of testing. Add to this a child's reluctance to perform for unfamiliar adults or in a strange environment and it becomes obvious that IQ tests may not always be a reliable or true indicator of ability.

Perhaps a better and more realistic way to describe the level of disability would be to categorize it according to its effect on the individual. While this is less rigid and, perhaps, more open to individual interpretation, it does provide a greater insight into both current achievement and future potential. According to this classification, those with a mild learning disability should grow up to lead a relatively normal life, although they may need help dealing with difficult situations. Those with a moderate learning disability will be capable of understanding and carrying out routine tasks but will generally require supervision and support on a daily basis. They will use simple language to communicate. A severe learning disability will impact further upon an individual's abilities and while some within this category will have the potential to perform basic everyday activities, they will require constant supervision if they are to succeed. Many will use signs or symbols to communicate. Children and adults with a profound learning disability will require the most care and attention. With the intellectual capacity of, perhaps, a baby or young child, they will need someone to look after their every need and to provide them with 24-hour care in all areas of their lives.

Causes of learning disabilities

The vast range of conditions that can cause a learning disability is wide and varied. In many cases the reason is obvious, while in others there is no known cause. In addition, some children may have a combination of intellectual, physical and sensory disabilities as well as emotional and behavioural difficulties. It is beyond the purpose of this book to delve into each and every condition; instead the causes will be broken down into three main areas, based on when they occur.

Prenatal causes of learning disabilities occur before birth. They are always present at birth and while some are immediately recognizable, others may not be diagnosed as easily. Examples of these include

- Chromosomal, genetic or inherited disorders such as Down's Syndrome or Fragile X
- Substance abuse (alcohol, nicotine, cocaine, etc.)
- Dietary deficiencies including iodine or folic acid deficiency, or severe malnutrition in the mother
- Exposure to harmful chemicals, medications or radiation
- Infections in the mother (rubella, syphilis, HIV, etc.)
- Complications in pregnancy such as heart disease, kidney disease or diabetes in the mother.

Perinatal causes occur at birth or during the neonatal period (the first four weeks of the child's life). Examples of these include

- Severe prematurity or very low birth weight
- Lack of oxygen during the birth process
- Difficult delivery
- Conditions in the baby such as severe jaundice or septicaemia.

Postnatal causes, occurring during infancy and childhood, may include

- Brain infections such as bacterial meningitis
- Head injury

◆ Nutritional deprivation
◆ Neglect
◆ Gross understimulation
◆ The MMR (measles, mumps, rubella) vaccine, which some controversially believe can be one of the causes of autism, also falls into this category, although there is still no conclusive evidence for this.

Whatever the cause, it is important to remember that a learning disability can never be cured. This is not to say that those affected will not make progress; on the contrary, almost all, with perhaps the possible exception of the few with the most acute profound and multiple learning difficulties, will learn new skills and develop social aptitudes. Many will learn to read and write, to form relationships, attend local colleges to further their education and to participate in voluntary or paid employment. Their learning disability will, however, remain with them throughout their life.

Within any one condition, varying levels of impairment can occur and some children will be affected more than others. This often makes it difficult to accurately predict the ultimate outcome of a learning disability. Two children born with Down's Syndrome, for example, may vary greatly in what they will eventually achieve. While one may learn to read, write, speak, and care for himself with minimal supervision, the other may struggle with these skills, relying on parents and carers to support him in almost all that he does. Other conditions may be more prevalent in, or almost exclusively confined to, one sex. Fragile X, for example, is an hereditary condition which not only affects more males than females, but which also leads to greater impairment among affected boys than girls.

> Tip! Remember that, just as non-disabled children born into one family will differ in their abilities, so will any group of children born with the same medical syndrome or condition.

Diagnosing a learning disability

The diagnosis of a learning disability, like the cause, can occur at almost any stage of a child's life. If the cause is a known hereditary condition, or if it has been detected through a scan or test during pregnancy, the parents of the developing baby may be faced with the difficult decision of whether or not to abort. Individual circumstances, religious beliefs and the perceived ability to cope with a disabled child all have an effect upon this purely personal decision, for which there is no right or wrong answer.

Most parents, however, are not aware of their child's learning disability until minutes, days, weeks or even years after the birth. In some cases, the disability may be immediately apparent, while in others it may only be diagnosed as the child grows and develops. Often it is only when the child does not meet normal developmental targets that the parents begin to worry. In a small number of cases, where the condition is degenerative, the learning disability may not be diagnosed until the child begins to lose previously acquired skills, including intellectual capabilities, communication, mobility and sensory skills.

The diagnosis of a learning disability may come from a variety of sources. In many cases, it will come directly from the medical profession when doctors, nurses, midwives and health visitors recognize early telltale signs or characteristics. However, the parents of children with mild or moderate learning disabilities, or with conditions that only become evident as the child fails to follow normal patterns of development, are often the first to suspect that their child may have some degree of learning disability. These parents often face a long, painful and slow diagnosis and some may spend several years trying to convince others of their concerns before a diagnosis is finally made.

Whenever and however the condition is diagnosed, parents will need time to adjust, to ask questions and to seek answers and information. They will need extra support, both emotionally and physically, to help them come to terms with the news that will, no doubt, affect them for the rest of their lives.

Life expectancy

Over the years, advances in medical science have led to an increased life expectancy for all members of society. It is expected that the majority of those born in the United Kingdom today will live well into their seventies or eighties and the number of those reaching their hundredth birthday continues to grow.

Similarly the majority of children with a learning disability can look forward to a long and healthy life. Improvements in medical and social care and increased awareness of the needs of people with learning, physical and sensory disabilities ensure that their needs are not only understood but, as far as possible, are also fully catered for. These factors are, among others, part of the reason that the Department of Health white paper (as described earlier, 2001) estimates that the number of people with severe learning disabilities may increase by around 1 per cent per year over the 15 years following its publication.

There are some children, however, whose degenerative disorder will lead to a gradual deterioration and to a shortened life expectancy. The prognosis for these children may vary according to the condition and while some may survive into their teens or beyond, others may not survive longer than several years. Those children born with profound and multiple learning difficulties may also have a shortened life expectancy. While their learning disabilities may not always affect their lifespan, accompanying physical disabilities may result in common ailments such as colds or chest infections proving too much for those who are not strong enough to fight them off.

Finally . . .

The information in this section has intentionally been kept brief and non-specific. For those who wish to learn more, particularly about particular conditions, information is available from a wide variety of sources, including literature from medical sources, charities and support groups, libraries and the internet.

2 | Effects of a learning disability upon the child

All cassavas have the same skin but not all taste the same.

–Kenyan proverb

Every one of us is different. We all have different likes and dislikes, different levels of concentration, perseverance and tolerance. Some are natural loners while others need to be surrounded by friends and family, and while the extroverts among us will happily chat to all and sundry, those less confident may shy away from social situations where they know they will be required to mix with large numbers of people.

In this respect, children with learning disabilities are no different. Despite the fact that, for some, their condition may determine certain characteristics, each and every one is unique. They will laugh and cry, feel happiness, sadness, excitement, fear, and pain like all other children. Compared to their non-disabled peers, though, children with learning disabilities will take longer to develop new ideas and concepts, may find relationships more difficult to establish and friendships may be more difficult to sustain.

Teachers, parents and carers of children with learning disabilities will, in some cases, need to rethink all they have learned about childcare and development. They may need to adapt, to plan ahead and to find new ways of carrying out even the simplest and most mundane tasks. Their patience and tolerance will be tested to the utmost. They may become frustrated by the children's obsessive behaviours and find themselves re-evaluating their whole lives as their priorities and plans change, often at a moment's notice and almost certainly over the longer term. On the other hand, the smallest achievements, which perhaps would go unnoticed if accomplished by the non-disabled child, will bring joy, excitement and celebration.

Any learning disability will affect the child in many different ways, some of which will be explored in this chapter. However, while different conditions will inevitably bring their own unique characteristics there are some traits that, as we will see, are common, to a greater or lesser degree, in many children.

Intellectual and cognitive ability

Perhaps the most obvious effect of any learning disability is its impact upon intellectual and cognitive development. A learning disability affects not only the child's ability to learn but also his ability to generalize and retain information, to use thought and understanding and to make sense of what is happening.

Different conditions often bring their own, well-documented learning disorders, and much is written about the way various conditions affect learning. It is well known, for example, that the autistic child finds it difficult to relate to others and that this difficulty is often accompanied by poor communication skills and varying degrees of learning impairment. Even among those diagnosed with the same condition or syndrome, no two children will learn in the same way or at the same level, and their learning potential is as varied as that of any other group of children.

A learning disability can affect not only how much or how quickly a child learns but also the way in which he learns. Some, described as having a global developmental delay, will follow normal learning patterns, with all areas of learning developing at a similar pace. The extent of the learning disabilities, though, will determine the rate at which these children develop. Others may have 'pockets' or 'islands' of learning that make the acquisition of knowledge more erratic and unpredictable. In the most extreme form of this type of learning disability there are children who, while being unable to read, write, or look after themselves on a daily basis can perform incredible mathematical feats or who are artistically or musically gifted. These individuals, commonly known as 'savants', (from the French verb 'savoir' meaning 'to know') are few and far between, with more males than females having the condition. Many children with a learning disability will, however, develop different skills at different rates although to a much lesser degree than those who make the headlines because of their unique skills.

> *Georgia, aged 15, was a prime example of a child who demonstrated pockets, or islands, of learning. She was unable to read or write, to relate what she had done the previous day or to talk about what she would to do during the weekend. She did, however, have a good general knowledge of the British royal family, including the names of many of the royals, their relationships with each other and where they lived. While her knowledge was not in any way exceptional, it far exceeded her abilities in all other areas and was learned, parrot-fashion, from books and articles read to her by her parents and by watching television programmes and news broadcasts about them. As Georgia developed, this interest became an obsession. Unfortunately, her learning disability prevented her from understanding that not everybody shared her enthusiasm. Eventually, many less tolerant people avoided conversation with Georgia, knowing that they would again be informed of the latest activities of this distinguished family.*

Another effect of a learning disability is an inability to generalize information or to transfer knowledge from one skill to another. Most of us are able to do this automatically, being able not only to draw upon existing knowledge but also to adapt it where necessary, applying it to different situations or using it to rectify different problems.

Rosie, aged 7, was able to match coloured plastic counters with ease, although when asked to do the same with pencils, building bricks or large plastic beads, she could not do so. 10-year-old Archie, meanwhile, could count coins to ten but not toy cars, dinosaurs or soldiers. The inability to transfer these skills had a knock-on effect on other areas of development. While Rosie was able to understand a request to get a sock from a drawer, her inability to generalize her colour matching skill prevented her from selecting all of the blue socks, even when she was shown one as an example. Similarly, Archie was able to count up to ten coins but was unable to count eight cups at drink time or count five biscuits left on a plate.

Tip! Just because a child has learned to complete a task with one set of equipment or toys don't expect him to be able to do it with all other equipment. It is sometimes necessary to start the teaching process all over again to develop this skill.

Our ability to learn begins from the day we are born and continues throughout our entire lives. The knowledge we acquire, however, is better maintained if we use it on a regular basis, and the more we repeat a skill the better we become at maintaining it. The French we learned at school, for example, soon becomes rusty if we do not keep using the language. However, even many years later, if we were to take a holiday to France, we might well surprise ourselves with how much of the language we can recall. Many children with learning disabilities are not able to recall information learned in the past in this same way, and the more severe the disability the less likelihood there is of such information being recalled.

4-year-old Molly's profound disability made learning slow. Despite this, she was learning to recognize familiar members of her classroom staff and, after many months of practise, could always select her bright red cup when given a choice of that cup or a cup of a different colour. Nevertheless, after a short spell in hospital and her subsequent convalescence at home, a period of just four weeks, she no longer recognized either her cup or the staff who worked with her on a daily basis. Although it took her only four weeks to lose these skills, it took her much longer to relearn them and it was almost six months before she regained what she had lost during her illness.

Tip! Remember, the more severe the disability, the more important it is to continually practise and refine skills. These skills will soon be lost if neglected.

Social and behavioural characteristics

No two people are the same, and even within the same family there can be a range of different personalities and dispositions. Some people are naturally happy with a bubbly and easy-going outlook to life while others are more serious or withdrawn. Children with learning disabilities are no different and all will have their own unique personalities. Ask anyone to describe a child with Down's Syndrome and almost certainly they will describe him as being happy and loving, since this is the image which is usually portrayed in both popular culture and the media. However, there are a small minority of Down's Syndrome children who are quiet and sullen, and who prefer their own company to that of those around them. (Many of these children are now increasingly being diagnosed as having autism in addition to the more obvious Down's Syndrome.) Similarly, while most with Angelman Syndrome display the characteristic happy personality with outbursts of frequent (and often inappropriate) smiles and laughter, the extent of this behaviour can vary among individuals.

Despite their very individual personalities, children with learning disabilities can display many common characteristics. Many may find it difficult, for example, to form relationships with even the closest family members or to establish and maintain friendships with children of their own age. The skills which most of us learn in childhood and which enable us to relate to those around us, to empathise with them and understand their point of view, may not come easily to those with a learning disability. In addition, possible problems with communication or a lack of interest or understanding in what is happening around them can make it more difficult for these children to establish and maintain even the simplest of relationships. Opportunities to mix with others, especially as the child gets older, can be few and far between, and parents, carers and teachers must often manufacture conditions in which children can learn to work and play together in order to establish and maintain these relationships.

Tip! Try to provide as many opportunities as possible to help children with learning disabilities mix with other children of their own age.

Many with learning disabilities are very trusting of others and do not learn to fear strangers in the same way as other children. Most become used to the demands and requests of a wide range of different professionals and are rewarded for doing as they are asked without questioning or resisting. Teachers, paediatricians, nurses, physiotherapists etc may be a part of everyday life and what some may regard as an intrusion into their personal space becomes the norm for these youngsters. They are often unable to distinguish between those whose aims are simply to help and those who have, perhaps, more sinister reasons for their attentions. A 14-year-old girl, for example, attending hospital for yet another check-up with an unfamiliar doctor may think nothing of a request to strip down to her underwear for a physical examination. On occasions, her own GP (general practitioner) or the school nurse may need to examine her to enable the correct diagnosis of physical symptoms while the school doctor, during his annual visit, may make similar requests. Additionally, her physiotherapist may need her to remove some clothing to enable her spine to be checked when assessing whether or not her daily exercise programme is helping her physical disability. What is the difference, then, between these requests and similar ones from the adult in charge of the after-school club, her sister's boyfriend or the person who looks after her each Saturday evening while her parents go out? Her lack of understanding of right and wrong – or her desire to please – could, potentially, place this girl, and others like her, in difficult and worrying situations.

All children need and flourish on routine and familiarity. The same bedtime story each night, the same way of lining toys up along a shelf or the same route to school each day are all essential parts of learning. These routines allow the child to know what is happening as well as what to expect next. For some with a learning disability, though, the need for routine is especially important.

Daisy, aged 8, knew the route that the family took each Sunday as they drove to her grandparents' house. The journey always began after lunch and followed the same route, passing the same familiar landmarks and making the same predictable twists and turns. However, due to a road closure, the family were forced, one day, to take a different route. While her younger brother and sister were able to understand that their destination would be the same despite the unfamiliarity of the roads, Daisy became upset and anxious as a result of her uncertainty. She began to have tantrums, lashing out and shouting uncontrollably; to her a different route meant that she was going to a different place. Her comfortable routine was shattered and it was not until she reached her destination that she finally began to calm down.

Similarly, in school, a change to the usual routine can cause distress among those who do not understand that changes will occur or why they will happen. For most children a visiting theatre group or a trip to a local park or museum, apart from being exciting in itself, may also mean a break from the usual maths or science lesson – an added bonus, perhaps, for some! The child with a learning disability, however, will not view this in the same way and, just as Daisy reacted to the change in her Sunday routine, a child in the classroom may react to changes by displaying similar behaviours. It is important, then, that, whenever possible, children are given information about what is happening in a way that they can readily understand.

Tip! Children with learning disabilities thrive on routine. Wherever possible, all changes should be clearly explained, both before and during the change.

Attention, concentration and motivation

We often hear people talk about attention or concentration spans or our ability to maintain interest in, or to persevere with, a task. These terms are frequently used at random despite the fact that the ability to attend differs from the ability to concentrate. We can attend to a noise or something that catches our eye even when we are doing other things. We may focus our attention on something for a short time without becoming directly involved with it. However, to concentrate on a task we must fully engage in it, sometimes to the exclusion of everything else. We can concentrate on physical as well as mental tasks, although we may find it more difficult to concentrate if we are tired, worried, bored or simply not interested in the task.

Almost all children with severe or profound learning disabilities will have shortened levels of attention and concentration. Along with this, motivation to learn, conform, cooperate or comply with the wishes of others may be low. The greater the disability the lower the levels of motivation are likely to be, with those children with profound and multiple learning difficulties being the most affected. In the most extreme cases, attention and concentration may be limited to a few seconds at most, which inevitably makes teaching a time-consuming and lengthy process.

> Tip! Use toys and equipment that interest the child. Motivation to perform will be greater which, in turn, leads to increased attention and concentration.

It is worth noting here that the lack of attention and concentration caused by a learning disability are different from those caused by Attention Deficit Hyperactivity Disorder (ADHD). This condition, which generally affects more boys than girls, can also result in hyperactivity, impulsiveness, restlessness, constant fidgeting, anxiety and even depression. It can affect children of all ages and abilities and, while some children with learning disabilities may be affected by it, ADHD itself is not a learning disability.

Challenging behaviour

All children misbehave at times; it is a normal part of growing up. However, occasionally this can become so severe that it is referred to as challenging behaviour. Such behaviour differs in intensity, frequency and duration from normal temper tantrums or outbursts and has the potential to harm not only the child but also adults, other children and pets, and to damage objects and possessions.

There are many reasons for the onset of challenging behaviour including pain, boredom, frustration, fear, anger or confusion. One particularly common cause, however, is related to the child's lack of communication skills. We, as fully functioning adults, can verbally vent our anger when we stub our toe on a piece of furniture. We are also capable of adapting our responses to suit the situation. In the classroom, surrounded by children, we may simply let out a squeal, in a public place we may display pain and anger ('ouch, that hurt!' or even 'what a stupid place to put a chair!'), while in the privacy of our own homes the language may be less restrained! The child with a severe learning disability and no formal communication skills has neither the understanding nor the language to be as controlled. He may throw the chair, lash out at people around or even hit himself in pain and anger. Now, if we had observed the incident, we would have understood the reasons for his behaviour. If not (and we cannot watch every child continually), we suddenly see a child behaving in an unacceptable way and label his response as 'challenging behaviour'.

There are no right or wrong ways of coping with this type of behaviour and responses will vary according to the child and the situation. The best way, when possible, is to try and foresee or pre-empt situations which may lead to displays of unacceptable or challenging behaviours. Failing this, some children may respond to distraction techniques, others may be motivated by a system of rewards to help them manage their behaviour, while in a few cases, it may be better to simply ignore the behaviour, providing that it causes no harm to either the child or others around him. In extreme cases, medication may be the only solution, but this should not be used until all other remedies have been exhausted, and even then only after a full and proper assessment.

Tip! Try using an ABC system to record challenging behaviours. By making a note of the **a**ntecedent (what happened before the behaviour started), the **b**ehaviours and the **c**onsequences, it may be possible to determine a common reason for the child's behaviour as well as helping to establish an early warning system to prevent it from reoccurring.

Finally . . .

As in the last chapter, the information stated here is very general and non-specific. Just as we are able to say 'many six-year-olds like to play on swings' we can also say 'many with learning disabilities will . . .'. We can make general statements about any group of children, young people or adults, in the same way as we have made sweeping statements here about children with learning disabilities. We must remember, though, that just as there are some children who do not enjoy playing on swings, or who will only go on swings which are a certain height or have seats of a certain colour, so children with learning disabilities will have their own specific characteristics and idiosyncrasies.

Do not expect every child to act or respond in the same way as others with the same condition. Similarly, do not expect that all children with a learning disability will behave in the same way. Expect to be surprised by each individual and you will not be disappointed.

Effects of a learning disability upon the family

Patience is the greatest of all virtues.

—Cato the Elder, Roman statesman (234–149 BC)

Having a family is, for most people, one of the joys of growing up. The love and care bestowed on each child from the very beginning can only be matched by the excitement of watching them grow, learn, become independent and finally go on to have children of their own. For many parents the possibility of having a child with a disability will, inevitably, cross their minds at some stage. These thoughts are often short-lived and, for most, unfounded. For some, however, their fears may become a reality. These parents will need to rethink their lives, making changes, perhaps, to their routines or lifestyles as the extra demands of the new baby begin to take over. At each stage of life new challenges will occur, not just throughout childhood but also throughout puberty, adolescence and the teenage years, until, eventually, the need to make long-term decisions regarding the needs of an adult with a learning disability begin to take over.

Receiving a diagnosis

From the moment a diagnosis of a learning disability is received, many parents will feel as though their world has been shattered. Those who receive this news during the highly emotional first few weeks after the birth may experience a wide range of emotions including confusion, shock, anger and sorrow. Some may also experience an overwhelming and fierce protectiveness of their child, while others, unable to cope with the diagnosis, may experience depression, denial or, occasionally, even rejection of their long-awaited infant Many may feel guilt and blame themselves as they struggle to understand the causes and consequences of their child's individual needs. Parents of toddlers or older children, for whom the diagnosis is received much later, may experience different emotions. Some will feel sadness, much akin to a bereavement, as they mourn the child they thought they had and it may take many months for these parents to begin to accept their 'new' child. Others, concerned that their child had not been developing in the same way as his peers, may feel relief that somebody has, at last, acknowledged that their fears and concerns about him are justified. Whenever the diagnosis is confirmed, and whatever the parent's feelings, these will, no doubt be mixed with worry for the child's future as they reflect upon the uncertainty that lies ahead as well as their own ability to cope with the increased demands of a learning disabled youngster. Undoubtedly, they will require extra support, both emotionally and physically, to help them come to terms with the news, as well as time to adjust, to ask questions and to seek answers and information.

Feelings aside, different people will cope with a diagnosis such as this in different ways; while some will simply take it in their stride and accept that their child may need extra help and support, others will make it their mission to read up about the condition, join self-help or support groups and endeavour to promote awareness of the condition. Fortunately, information on many conditions and contact details for support groups are now freely available online and a list of useful websites can be found at the end of this book.

Tip! Don't be surprised to find some parents still feeling guilty, anxious or upset about their child's learning disabilities many years after the diagnosis.

From tots to teens

Coping with an infant or young child with learning disabilities brings with it many worries, concerns and problems as well as much satisfaction, pride and pleasure. However, parents of children with a learning disability may have to adapt to a new and often unfamiliar way of life. Initially, they may need support and guidance to help them cope with their new baby. As he grows, so may the number of support workers involved in his care, and this list could include, among others, paediatricians, physiotherapists, occupational therapists, speech and language therapists, dieticians, ophthalmologists, audiologists and educational psychologists. In addition, the parents may also receive home visits from their social worker and, later, the pre-school support teacher. In fact the more profound the disability, the greater this list becomes. While many parents will welcome this extra support, some may resent this intrusion into their lives and their whole routine often turns upside down as they struggle to fit in simple everyday commitments.

At some time during the child's infancy many parents may consider joining a toddler group, nursery group or pre-school playgroup. However, worries about how they will cope with the stares, comments, disapproving looks or pitying glances from others may prevent some parents from doing so. Even in today's enlightened age, some adults are embarrassed to talk to parents of learning disabled children, fearing that they may say something to upset them. Children, on the other hand, are much freer in their comments and will, as any parent knows, ask questions without thought, prejudice or malice.

2-year-old Willow and her mum regularly attended a pre-school playgroup at the local church hall. Her learning and physical disabilities were obvious to the other parents who understood her limited capabilities and while they freely accepted her into the group, they did not discuss Willow's disabilities with their own children. Things changed one day, though, when a little boy approached his mum and asked 'Mummy, why can't Willow walk or talk like me?' His mum blushed with embarrassment and glanced across to check whether Willow's mum had overheard. 'Ssh', she said, 'You don't ask questions like that'. Willow's mum, however, called the boy over. 'You know sometimes how you fall over and your knee is poorly' she said, 'Well, Willow's brain is poorly. It might take a long time to get better, not like your knee, but one day she might be able to walk and talk just like you'. Satisfied with this answer, the boy walked back to his friends and carried on playing.

The little boy in the story above had just turned three years of age. It is commonly believed that children below this age do not generally notice differences between themselves and others. In Willow's case, however, her disabilities were particularly noticeable; had she had less severe learning and physical disabilities it is questionable whether he would have even noticed at all.

Long before the parents of non-disabled children think about their child starting school, those with learning disabled children will need to consider which type of school will be the best for their child. Currently in the UK most will attend either state-run mainstream or special schools, although, increasingly, some will split their education between the two. However, the decision is not easy and parents will have to consider many options. Will the child learn quicker, for example, from his peers in a class of perhaps 30 other children, or will the smaller classes of a special school, with a higher staff ratio, be more able to meet his needs? Will he be better placed within his own locality where local children (and their parents) will learn to know and understand his individual needs and behaviours better? Can he cope with the journey to the nearest or most suitable special school, bearing in mind that this may be much farther away than the closest primary school? Will there be an opportunity to transfer to a special school if mainstream education becomes inappropriate? For those whose children have profound and multiple learning difficulties the decision may be less difficult since very few mainstream schools will be able to provide the specialized equipment or professional staffing their child requires. Parents of children with less severe disabilities, however, will need to face up to these decisions, often at a time when they are still confused and bewildered about what the future will hold. They will need to apply for, and obtain, a Statement of Special Educational Needs from their local education authority outlining the child's needs and specifying the most appropriate type of school, often a long and time-consuming process. As one parent once put it 'Talk about kick me while I'm down!'

> Tip! See Chapter 13 for more about the Statement of Special Educational Needs.

Once the child starts school his parents will need to adapt to a new routine without their child at home. This especially affects those parents who may have given up work to care for their severely or profoundly disabled child. Having spent each day looking after his every need, some may find their days long and empty. Others, perhaps those with additional family or work commitments, will welcome this new routine with open arms. They will all, however, begin to see the gap widen between their own child and those children without learning disabilities. The parents may only be able to look on as other children start to read, write and make friends of their own. Those whose children attend special schools, perhaps many miles away, will also miss the companionship of other local parents. They will not be able to socialize with local parents meeting at the school gates at the end of each day or at local events such as school sports days, assemblies or summer fetes.

Parents who have elected to send their child to a mainstream school may need to regularly review whether this continues to remain the most suitable option. The child's intellectual, cognitive and social development as well as the relevance of the curriculum and the school's ability to meet his needs must all be considered. While some children will continue their education alongside their non-disabled peers, many parents transfer their child at seven or, more frequently, eleven years of age when a change of school would happen regardless of ability. Now, instead of the pleasure and anticipation of seeing their child enter this exciting new phase of their life many parents are faced with the realization, once again, that he will not progress in the same way or as quickly as his non-disabled peers.

> Tip! Some children will be better placed in the local primary school, while others will benefit more from a special school placement. Each decision must be made with the needs of the individual child in mind.

From a teenager to an adult

During their teenage years non-disabled children will begin to develop their own interests and friendships and, gradually, as they start to make decisions for themselves, they will become more independent and less reliant on others. They start to socialize more, perhaps going swimming with friends, taking the bus into town or simply meeting up to share the latest gossip. Later, they may study for traditional examinations or vocational qualifications, learn to drive, secure a job or accept a place at university. Most will, at some point, leave home and settle into a long-term relationship or marriage. Parents of young people with learning disabilities can only watch as the gap between non-disabled children and their own children widens even further. As the following story shows, for these parents, even simple decisions, such as whether or when to allow their child out unaccompanied, can be fraught with worry.

Every year Davyn, aged 19, spent the entire summer holidays with his family in a small coastal village in western Scotland. Having holidayed there for many years, they were well known in the community and they considered the area as their 'second home'. It was here, in these small, friendly surroundings that they eventually decided to allow Davyn to walk by himself to the local village store. With no major roads to cross and a walk of only a few minutes, they hoped it would give them the confidence to allow him to go out unaided once he returned home. Determined to increase his independence, they practised the route together and ensured he was able to cross the road safely. Then, putting the worry of his unusual gait and his habit of staring directly at people to the back of their minds, they sent him off to buy some milk.

All went well, and Davyn returned home ten minutes later with his shopping. His parents were thrilled, as much for themselves as their son. They felt their time and patience had finally paid off, and that he had now taken one more step to independence. His trips out became more frequent and, as time progressed, he was allowed to stay out a little longer. Until the day he returned home accompanied by a police officer who told how a local mum, new to the area, had seen Davyn standing and watching her daughter as she played in the garden.

Being suspicious and not knowing of Davyn's learning disability, she had called the police. Davyn eventually admitted that he had been watching the little girl purely because he wanted to be her friend. He then went on, unexpectedly, to tell how he had also been taunted by a group of local teenagers who jeered at him for always being alone as well making fun of his unusual way of walking. His parents were devastated. Mixed with their feelings of anger, concern and disappointment were feelings of guilt that they had, in some way, failed their son.

The situation described above is, perhaps, most applicable to those parents whose children have a mild or moderate learning disability since those with a more severe disability, not understanding that others their age have these opportunities and experiences, will not generally yearn for similar freedoms. However, there is one stage through which all teenage children pass, regardless of their ability: puberty. This stage, beginning on average between the ages of ten and twelve and lasting approximately three to four years, can transform even the calmest and most placid youngster into one who is stubborn, moody, demanding, uncooperative or verbally abusive. Most parents of non-disabled teenage children will readily admit that these years are equally as difficult as those spent rearing a baby or small toddler, although for obviously different reasons. Now imagine how difficult this time must be for young people with learning disabilities as well as for their families. Despite the fact that they may be functioning at a young age intellectually, their body is rapidly changing into that of an adult, and puberty, being a physical process, will occur as normal. In contrast to this, normal developmental stages can occur at different ages depending on the severity of the disability. However, for some of these children and their families, a combination of physical and developmental stages can be particularly demanding as the following story demonstrates.

Samuel, aged 14, was a big, well-built young man with a severe learning disability. At the age of 9 he was functioning, on average, at the level of a two-year-old. His language was progressing in accordance with his developmental age, his mobility was good and, much to his parents' joy, he was starting to show some signs of independence. Gradually, though, his parents noticed that his behaviour was starting to change and he would stamp his feet, fall to the floor or shout and scream in a bid to get his own way. These behaviours were often displayed in public, much to the embarrassment of his parents who began to dread taking him out for fear of what other people would think. Desperate for help, they talked to their GP, and were told he was simply displaying the normal developmental behaviours associated with the 'terrible twos'. However, unlike non-disabled children who pass through this stage relatively quickly, it took

*Samuel almost four years to pass through it, bringing him to 13 years of age . . .
and then puberty struck!*

Having learning disabilities meant that Samuel, and consequently his
whole family, suffered the 'terrible twos' much later and for much longer
than non-disabled children. However, just as these behaviours began to
subside, those related to puberty took over, extending the period of unpredictable behaviour by several more years.

> Tip! Expect the terrible twos to occur at any age since they are
> related to a developmental stage rather than to chronological
> age. Puberty, however, will almost always occur during the
> teenage years, regardless of ability.

Linked to puberty, of course, is a growing awareness of the opposite sex and
all the feelings and frustrations that accompany this. Often unable to understand their own feelings, and with the mind of a child but the sexual feelings of
an adult, the young person may display inappropriate behaviours in public.
They may also develop sexual feelings towards others of a similar age, an
entirely normal behaviour but one that frequently comes as a shock to parents
who perhaps had not expected it. It is often only at this point that they start to
think about some form of sex education and to consider how, with their child's
understanding limited to the here and now, he will cope with this. Their heads
will, no doubt, be full of questions about what to say, when and how to say it,
how much will be understood or even who should teach it. Fortunately sex education forms part of the curriculum in most mainstream and special schools, and
careful and sensitive programmes are developed to help deal with this subject.
This is not to say that parents can relinquish this responsibility and, like all forms
of education, sex education is most successful when it is taught at home as well
as in school. No matter how good the programme appears, though, sex education is, perhaps, one of the most difficult areas to teach, as this story, of unknown
origin but told one day in a school staffroom, demonstrates.

*After leaving school at 19, Peter and Beth, both with moderate to severe learn-
ing disabilities, left home and moved into residential accommodation. It
wasn't long before staff started to notice a close friendship blossoming between
them and soon they were observed spending more and more time in each other's rooms. Although both Peter and Beth had participated in a sex education*

programme at school, which was backed up by parental involvement at home, it was decided that they would benefit from a few more sessions, with particular reference this time to contraception. Both sets of parents were consulted and both took an active part during the sessions. Once complete, everyone felt that both young people were fully aware of the consequences of unprotected sex and their relationship was allowed to flourish.

Soon afterwards, though, Beth's periods stopped. She was given a pregnancy test that confirmed that she was, indeed, pregnant. Shocked, the staff approached Peter. 'Why didn't you use a condom as we taught you?' they asked. Peter was adamant in his reply, insisting that he was always very careful and he really couldn't understand why Beth was pregnant.

Some time later, the relationship ended and Peter found himself a new girlfriend. Aware of the past, both Peter's parents as well as his carers talked to him again about contraception. Things went well until one morning Peter and his new girlfriend overslept and staff went to check on them. It was only then that they realised their talks about contraception had not been fully understood and there, on his bedside table, was a courgette proudly wearing a condom!

Whether or not this story is true, it demonstrates how difficult it is to teach young people with learning disabilities the facts about sex education. Is it any wonder, then, that parents worry about what and how to tell their teenage children about this? Peter had, as he had accurately insisted, done everything he had been taught. His inability to realize that the courgette was merely a teaching aid placed him, as well as his parents and carers, in a very difficult situation as they pondered how to find other, more relevant and appropriate ways of getting the necessary information across.

> Tip! Encourage communication between home and school about the best way to teach sex education to children with learning disabilities.

As young people with learning disabilities reach their late teens, many parents begin to worry about what will happen or how they will cope as they themselves become older and less able to offer the full-time care that many young people with learning disabilities require. While the usual expectation that their child will leave home, find a job or go to university does not necessarily apply to parents of learning disabled children, there are now an increasing number of options available depending upon the extent of the disability. Some young people may remain in the family home while others may move into homes or centres in the community where they can live as independently as possible, while being continually supervised by a team of live-in carers. Those with moderate or severe disabilities may attend day centres or local colleges where there are an increasingly wide variety of courses available, while the lucky few may find employment on a part-time or even full-time basis. Parents of young adults with profound and multiple learning difficulties, however, have fewer choices available to them. They may find that residential homes, with their ability to provide the comprehensive twenty-four hour care that their children require, are often the most appropriate option.

Tip! Whatever the ability of the young person and whatever choices are made, it is vital that parents begin to plan for this well ahead of time. By beginning this process early, they can ensure that he will be settled into a happy and comfortable routine as they, themselves, eventually become unable to cope with the on-going continuous care that is often necessary.

Changes to family life

So far in this chapter we have considered the worries and emotions faced by parents of learning disabled children. Many parents, though, will also need to consider the practical aspects of family life and to find ways of allowing their child to continue to live as normally as possible despite his disability. Depending upon the extent of their disability, children with learning disabilities will require a great deal of time and care. Unlike their non-disabled counterparts, though, they may continue to need this for many years. The usual morning routine for most school-aged children, for example, will find them washing and dressing themselves, helping themselves to breakfast, cleaning their teeth and packing their bag with, perhaps, just a few reminders or words of encouragement. These simple tasks, which most are able to do independently by the age of six or seven, may never be achieved by those with severe or profound learning disabilities or, if they are, may take much longer to both learn and complete. To cope with this, parents may need to reorganize an already busy daily schedule and to be flexible in their own routine not just at the start of the day but often until, tired and exhausted by their efforts, they finally put the child to bed.

In addition to the changes in daily routine, hospital or clinic appointments may interrupt the weekly or monthly routine. The career or work life of a parent may be affected as he or she takes time off to attend such appointments as well as to care for their child. In some cases, it may be necessary to give up work completely. Such a decision has financial implications which, in addition to the stress often associated with caring for a learning disabled child, can occasionally lead to marital problems or even a total breakdown of the relationship. To add to this accumulated stress, the family home may need to be adapted to meet the needs of a growing child. Sometimes this adaptation may be as simple as rearranging living areas to allow the storage of essential equipment or to provide a calming, stimulating or clutter-free environment. Those whose children have profound and multiple learning difficulties may have to consider the addition of a downstairs bedroom and bathroom, widening doorways to allow wheelchair access or the fitting of lifts and hoists to reduce the amount of lifting required as he grows in both size and weight. In addition, the family car may need changing (or perhaps a second car may need to be purchased), perhaps to one that will accommodate a wheelchair or allow easier access for a child with limited mobility.

Simple, everyday activities and outings will almost certainly require extra planning and preparation. The excitement shown by a non-disabled child when he goes on a special day out or leaves home for a week's holiday is replaced in the learning disabled child, by confusion as he struggles anxiously to understand what is happening to his normal, everyday routine. On arrival at their chosen destination, the family may have to cope with a child who displays challenging behaviours or does not conform to the behaviour codes generally expected in public places. Even a simple trip to the cinema, for example, can be difficult if the child does not understand the boundaries or the simple, unwritten rules of society to which we all adhere. Lack of attention and concentration, uncontrolled shouting, crying or verbal demands, or, for mobile children, an inability to stay seated for any length of time, can all contribute to making the trip difficult for the whole family. Other families, however, may have different problems to consider. Those whose children have profound and multiple learning difficulties may need to check that any necessary medication is organized beforehand, that the child can be fed and can be given a drink (often via a feeding tube directly into the stomach), and that the venue has both wheelchair access and changing facilities suitable for older children should these be required.

Given the extra time required to care for a child with learning disabilities, it is little wonder that the family rarely has the time to relax and enjoy the everyday activities which most of us enjoy. Fortunately, many families are able to access respite care facilities, enabling them to enjoy what some would call a 'normal' family life, free from the pressures and stresses associated with looking after a child with learning disabilities. These facilities, generally available through Social Services, voluntary and charitable groups or through private arrangement, provide short-term care in hospitals, hospices, residential establishments or in the home of the child or provider. As well as providing a welcome break for the family and a range of exciting activities designed to suit the individual needs of each child, this can also prepare him for the time when he may inevitably need to leave the family home and live in other accommodations that are better suited to his needs, age and ability.

The effect on siblings

Having a brother or sister with a learning disability can have an effect not just on the parents, but also on the siblings. It is not unusual for them to experience a wide range of emotions ranging from pride and protectiveness to anger and frustration. These feelings, similar in many ways to those of newly diagnosed parents, may persist for many years, changing frequently with age and circumstance. They may also experience resentment and jealousy; feelings which are completely normal and which are, at times, present in most families regardless of whether or not one of the children has a learning disability. Some may envy the attention the learning disabled child demands from the parents, while others may resent the lack of a normal family life. They may watch as their friends' families go out as a complete unit. Meanwhile, their own outings may split the family as one parent stays at home to look after their learning disabled sibling. Even in the home they may need to behave differently from their non-disabled friends, perhaps tidying toys away on an all too frequent basis to prevent them being damaged by a child with challenging behaviours or having to sit through endless repeats of a television programme just to keep their learning disabled sibling happy. In some cases, feelings of embarrassment and awkwardness may stop them from having even their closest friends to visit.

> From when he was tiny, Jacob, aged 15, had an aversion to wearing clothes and would strip off at any opportunity. As he grew, he learned to accept that he had to wear his clothes in public, but, on returning home, he would immediately discard them. This was accepted by the family while he was young, but became more of a problem as his body changed from that of a boy to a young man. His sisters in particular found this embarrassing, to the extent that, by the age of 12, they had stopped bringing female friends home. Several years later, they were also reluctant to bring boyfriends home when they knew Jacob would be present. Later they admitted that, despite understanding Jacob's unusual behaviours, they not only felt different from their friends but also that their own teenage years had been difficult because of Jacob's obvious dislike of wearing clothes in the home.

Jacob's sisters were obviously concerned about their friends' reaction to his behaviour, worrying that they would not understand it or, even worse, would misinterpret it. Fortunately, though, there are now an increasing number of clubs, many of which are run by charities, which offer support and understanding to siblings of children with severe or profound learning disabilities. These clubs allow children of all ages to meet and play together, share experiences and, most important, to have the opportunity to talk through their feelings with people in a similar position and who understand their feelings. An increasing number of special schools are now also setting up their own sibling support groups, which give people like Jacob's sisters a chance to meet locally with other young people in similar situations. An added bonus of these groups is, perhaps, that they provide the opportunity for the non-disabled siblings to experience some of the same activities that their learning disabled siblings experience on a regular basis. How many non-disabled children have, for example, spent time in a multi-sensory room, enjoyed the sensation of lying on a full-length vibrating bed or mattress, or relaxed with friends in a warm, soothing spa pool while being surrounded by soft music and gently glowing lights?

> Tip! Never underestimate the effect a learning disabled child can have on family life.

Finally . . .

Having a son, daughter, sister or brother with a learning disability can affect all aspects of traditional family life, and, for some families, life as they know it may never be the same again. Each stage of the child's life will bring new challenges to parents and siblings alike. There may be emotional, physical and, in some cases, financial pressures to face, tears and tantrums to contend with, and joy and celebration at each small, but highly significant achievement. Tolerance and patience will increase as the family adjusts to a new and different way of life. Despite these changes, however, it is important for everyone that family life is kept as normal as possible. After all, having a child with a learning disability does not stop brothers and sisters from wanting help with their homework, a cuddle when they fall or a bedtime story each night, nor parents from wanting a meal out with friends once in a while.

For those in education, it is important to remember that the child with a learning disability at school continues to be a child with a learning disability at home. An understanding of some of the problems faced by parents and siblings will help develop a more complete picture of the child which, in turn, will help not only in the planning but also in the delivery of a suitable and relevant curriculum to meet each child's very individual needs.

4 | Profound and multiple learning difficulties

Education is the kindling of a flame, not the filling of a vessel.
    –Socrates, ancient Greek philosopher (469–399 BC)

Children with profound and multiple learning difficulties have the most severe of all learning disabilities. On a sliding scale of disability, ranging through mild, moderate, severe and profound, those with profound and multiple learning difficulties face the biggest challenges in life. Their conditions are complex, affecting not only intellectual development, but also, as we shall see later, development in many other areas. They are totally dependent on others for all their needs. Many are unable to feed independently, most are doubly incontinent and some require assistance even to move or change position. A large percentage will also have complex medical needs that, in the past, would have resulted in their not surviving longer than a few weeks, months or years. However, as medical science advances, an increasing number of these children live longer, more fulfilling lives. As this chapter will explain, their needs, then, are very different in many ways to others with less complex learning disabilities.

What are profound and multiple learning difficulties?

In addition to having the severest of all learning disabilities, many children with profound and multiple learning difficulties also have physical and sensory impairments, hence the term 'profound and multiple'. The combination and level of disabilities make each individual unique. This is perhaps more true of children with profound and multiple learning difficulties than it is of those within any other category of learning disability.

As well as affecting intellectual progress and development, a profound learning disability also affects the child's ability to compensate for, and to overcome, any sensory or physical disability. A child whose sole disability is visual, for example, will make more use of other senses. He will learn to use his fingers to read Braille, recognize faces by touch or be able to identify people approaching by the sound of their footsteps, skills that those with a profound learning disability may be unable to achieve. Similarly, those born with purely physical disabilities, or who suffer these as a result of accident or illness, will struggle to overcome them, to learn to walk (perhaps for the second time) or to hold a spoon to feed themselves. Imagine how difficult life must be for those who suffer not only sensory or physical disabilities but have, in addition, a profound learning disability. Without the ability to think things through, to plan ahead, to concentrate and persevere and to understand that their actions can change things – 'If I do this, that will happen' – they will find it difficult to compensate for, and to overcome, other disabilities.

In addition to this, communication will undoubtedly be affected. Few will be able to either use or understand the spoken word, relying instead on less conventional forms of communication. Some will develop the ability to use and understand simple communication systems such as *Objects of Reference* or the *Picture Exchange Communication System (PECS)*. Others may simply eye point, using their eyes to indicate preferences in the same way as we might use our fingers, gesture or speech, or may rely on others to interpret their facial expressions or movements. The communication system used will vary according to the abilities of each individual, and must be selected according to their intellectual, sensory and physical abilities. These, and other alternate forms of communication suitable for those with profound and multiple learning difficulties will be discussed further in Chapter 8.

Tip! Try to imagine what it must be like to have a profound and multiple learning difficulty. How many everyday activities will cease to be possible? What will you miss most? How will you interact with others? Try to remember these feelings when working with children with this type of disability.

Physical abilities

Children with profound and multiple learning difficulties have varying levels of physical abilities. While some are fully mobile and are able to walk, run and climb as well as any other child, the majority are confined to a wheelchair. The level and type of physical disability will vary from one child to the next. In some, for example, the whole body, including arms, legs, trunk and even head will be affected, while others may have use of their arms and upper body but not legs or lower body. Some will have little control over their movements and be permanently 'on the wriggle', while others will have almost no movement, with limbs almost locked into position. Most will receive visits from the physiotherapist and occupational therapist to help them make the most of any gross and fine motor skills and to advise on exercises and activities to be carried out between visits. They will also ensure that each child receives the correct equipment to make the most of his abilities as well as to aid in the development of new skills. This list of equipment generally increases along with the severity of the physical disability and may include hand, foot or leg splints, gaiters, orthotic boots, outdoor and indoor wheelchairs, specialized chairs and tables for school use, standing frames, supportive wedges for floor sitting and a range of specially-designed equipment aimed at the developing upper body control and unsupported sitting. (This list is not exhaustive and will undoubtedly include other equipment depending upon the child's requirements.)

Wheelchairs for those with profound and multiple learning difficulties are usually individually tailored to meet the child's specific needs, providing support for the head, neck and body, as well as being essential for mobility. However, of the many children in this group required to use a wheelchair, only a small minority will learn to control and manoeuvre it themselves. Those who do often take many months or years to develop this skill, and progress will inevitably be slow. A strong motivating factor will inevitably be needed and this, in itself, requires a certain level of anticipation and understanding. Consider the example of a wheelchair user who is able to move independently to the dining area at lunchtime. To do this, the ability to control a wheelchair, steering it through doorways or around people and objects is required, as well as the ability to understand the concept of 'lunchtime'. This understanding may take the form of the spoken or signed word (i.e. 'lunch' or 'dinner') or perhaps a picture, symbol or object which represents this. Alternatively, he may learn to interpret other signs such as the smell coming from the kitchen indicating that a meal is almost ready, or the rumbles coming from his empty tummy that mean that it is time to eat. Motivation enough for some, perhaps, but this motivation must also be accompanied by patience and perseverance by all if he is to master this difficult skill.

Children in wheelchairs may have fewer opportunities to develop and use the skills that they have already acquired or are in the process of learning. Consider the following example of two children, both with profound and multiple learning difficulties, who had been working hard at greeting familiar people by smiling, eye contact and attempts at vocalization.

Ella and Thomas, both 6 years old, had returned to their classroom after participating in the school Christmas concert. After a few minutes, their mums entered the room, chatting as they did so about what they had just seen. Engrossed in conversation, they did not see the attempts of their children to gain their attention. Neither child was able to call out, but both desperately smiled in their direction and tried hard to gain eye contact with them. Attempts at vocalization were

drowned out by the noise of other children and the CD player blaring out Christ-
mas music. After some time, Ella slid off her seat and bottom-shuffled towards
her mum, tugging at her clothes and smiling up at her to let her know she was
there. She was rewarded for her efforts with a big smile and a cheery hello before
being picked up and cuddled. Thomas, on the other hand, was less fortunate;
confined to his wheelchair, he was unable to gain his mum's attention, and she
continued her conversation for several minutes before walking across the room to
greet him.

While both Ella and Thomas struggled to initiate an interaction with their
mums, it was only Ella who, on this occasion, succeeded. The restriction placed
upon Thomas by his lack of mobility meant that, despite his best efforts, the
skills he had spent many months practising went unnoticed.

Children who are mobile also generally have more opportunities to explore
and learn from their environment than those who are confined to a wheelchair.
However this mobility also brings with it an element of risk. Those with profound learning difficulties often show no fear; they are unaware of the dangers
of climbing too high, squeezing through a gap in a hedge or walking into a
busy road. Their inability to reason or to learn from previous mistakes may
find them repeating the same potentially dangerous action many times over.
They may wander off from parents or carers, unknowingly putting themselves
in danger from local environmental hazards and also from the small minority
of people who will prey on others for their own gratification. Care must be
taken to ensure that these children are well supervised at all times to prevent
them from coming to any harm.

> Tip! Remember that a physical disability is not just an inability
> to walk or move unaided. A severe physical disability can affect
> many other areas of development.

Single sensory impairments

In addition to their learning disabilities and possible physical impairment,
many children with profound and multiple learning difficulties also suffer
impairments to one or more of the senses. This generally affects either vision or
hearing, although in some cases both of these senses can be affected. Sensory
impairments, in addition to a learning disability, can greatly impact upon a
child's learning capacity, as we shall see in this section.

Vision enables us to learn from our surroundings. It is perhaps our major
source of information, and, apart from those times when we simply close our

eyes or when we are asleep, it constantly keeps us informed about what is happening around us. With a field of vision extending to approximately 180 degrees, we are able to see much more than we actually realize. This wide visual field enables us, for example, to watch television but still be aware of what our children are doing while they play quietly on the floor beside us. We combine our central vision (in this case to watch television) and our peripheral vision (to keep us informed of what our children are doing) to provide us with essential information. We also use our vision to learn new tasks, and by watching others we are able to develop new talents and skills. Socially, we use our vision to recognize and greet friends, even those who may be across a crowded room or on the other side of the street. A passing stranger may smile at us and we acknowledge this by smiling back; a brief unspoken interaction that would not be possible without the use of vision. We are also able to see, recognize and memorize the way people, objects, and places look. Assuming we have an understanding of language we are able to visualize things that friends and family tell us when they describe what they have seen, what they are doing or where they are going. Consider, for example, the following statement:

> The sea was the deepest azure blue, with little white sailing boats bobbing on the horizon. Shoals of tiny fish darted around in the shallow water and a little fair-haired girl giggled as she jumped over the tiny white waves which broke silently on to the soft, golden sand.

Reading this, most of us are able to conjure up a picture of an idyllic day at the seaside. We are able to piece together the individual elements of the statement based on what we have seen in the past and what we are able to visually recall and then use this to mentally reproduce a picture in our minds. However, these words would mean little to us if we had never seen the sea, didn't know what a fish looked like or had no concept of colour.

Imagine, then, how difficult life must be for children who have impaired sight. With little or no vision, they will not be able to learn by watching and copying others, and simple activities may take longer to complete. They may be unaware of what is happening around them and will have trouble finding their way around all but the most familiar of environments. Social skills will take longer to develop and eye contact, an important element of communication, may never develop. Many words may lack meaning, and conversational skills will be slow to develop. They will appear to live in their own little worlds and may show little interest in others, including parents or other children. Perhaps surprisingly, some may show little or no response to a sudden or loud noise (except for reflex actions) and may not turn to find out what caused it; after all, why bother to turn to a sound when you can't see who or what is making it?

Hearing is our second major sense but, unlike vision, we are unable to switch this off. We are aware of sounds even in our sleep and awake to the sound of an early morning call or a baby crying. Whether or not we take notice of the sounds we hear depends upon many factors including what we are doing, our state of alertness or even the sound itself. It also depends on our interests; many of us would stop what we are doing to answer a ringing phone but, while being aware of it, would ignore birdsong coming from the garden. Someone with an interest in ornithology, however, might choose to ignore the phone but drop everything to follow the birdsong and catch a glimpse of the songbird outside. Similarly, while we may elect to ignore the sounds of people chatting in another room, it is often comforting to know that other people are around; it makes us feel secure and can take away feelings of loneliness. We learn to put meaning to sounds we hear, and from this we can anticipate what will happen; a child may learn that a key in the door means that Gran has arrived and that she will bring with her a listening ear, a big hug and a bit of extra attention! Hearing also alerts us to potential danger; a fire alarm, a car backing out of a drive or a call to 'Take care!' mean nothing unless we can hear and understand these warnings.

Hearing is essential, of course, for the development of language and children with impaired hearing will almost certainly suffer from delayed language and communication skills. They may not hear as those around them use spoken words to communicate and, consequently, will not learn to copy these words or use them in conversation. Alternatively, they may have some level of hearing, but the sounds they hear may be distorted. For these children, words as we know them may sound very different and, in return, we may struggle to understand any attempts by them to replicate and use even the simplest of words. Lacking the ability to use the spoken word, most will struggle to communicate in a world dominated by those with hearing. They will not receive the verbal feedback necessary for the formation of those first important words and will learn neither their own name nor the names of people and objects around them. Simple commands and requests from parents or carers will not be heard and the resulting lack of response can have devastating or harmful effects. Some may learn to sign and this will become their first language, but it will be of no value unless those around them also learn this new form of communication. They may feel isolated from the family group as those around them talk among themselves, and unless all members of the family use sign as their first language, the children will miss out on the general 'chit chat' which occurs in all households.

Tip! Try to encourage all members of the family to learn to sign and to use this regularly at home.

Dual sensory impairments

The term 'deafblind' is used to describe anyone who has impairments to both vision and hearing. It does not necessarily imply total blindness or total deafness, but rather that the person has some degree of impairment to both of these senses. The implications of these impairments, on top of a profound learning difficulty, are immense. Having both visual and auditory impairments affects other senses, as we shall see later.

> Tip! A child who has been diagnosed as deafblind may have some useful vision and/or hearing. Deafblind implies that there is impairment to both of these senses rather than complete blindness or deafness.

If, as it is often said, a lack of vision isolates people from the world and a hearing impairment cuts them off from those around them, imagine how much more challenging life must be if both vision and hearing are affected. Add to this a profound learning disability and you will begin to appreciate how difficult it is for children with profound and multiple learning difficulties to make sense of the world around them.

Stefan, aged 12 months, suffered from profound and multiple learning difficulties as well as impairments to both vision and hearing and was classified as deafblind. As he lay quietly in his cot, awareness of any external stimuli was reduced to a minimum and he had no concept of his surroundings. Having no knowledge of his mother entering the room to change his nappy, it came as a total shock to be suddenly lifted out of a warm, comfortable cot and placed on a cold, plastic changing mat. Not being aware of what was happening, he showed his shock and fear in the only way he knew how – by crying. This simple but necessary activity not only distressed Stefan but also upset his mother who worried that every time she touched her baby, he cried. She began to question her ability to care for her child, and the bond that naturally exists between parent and child was slow to develop.

Now compare Stefan's response to that of the non-impaired baby and his parent. Here, the infant will see and hear his mother entering the room. The mother will smile and speak as she approaches the cot, and in return, he will gurgle and wriggle with excitement. As she picks him up she will continue to make small talk and he will smile and look into her eyes. After being placed on the changing mat, the routine activity of nappy changing may develop into a few minutes of play, again with both seeking and maintaining eye contact with each other, as well as possible attempts by the baby to vocalize back as the adult continues to chat or sing. What is a natural and pleasurable experience for the non-impaired baby is, in contrast, a fearful and frightening one for the child with sensory impairments.

Multi-sensory impairments

With restricted sight and hearing, those who suffer from both a visual and auditory impairment must rely on the sense of touch to learn about the world around them. While deafblind children who do not have a learning disability learn to trust those around them, those with profound and multiple learning difficulties are often not able to develop this trust as readily. Consequently, they remain fearful of tactile activities. Take a simple early exploratory activity such as sand or water play. Most children will play happily in sand or water, copying others and learning new skills and concepts through experimentation, trial and error and repetition. However, the child with dual sensory impairments in addition to a profound learning disability may show very different responses to those of his non-impaired peers. Just as Stefan, isolated in his own world, demonstrated what appeared to be negative reactions when suddenly lifted out of his cot, the older child, perhaps seated in a wheelchair and unaware of what is about to happen, will react when his hands are suddenly placed into a bowl of cold, wet sand. In this case, a cry of protest will usually be accompanied by him pulling his hands sharply out of the sand, and actively resisting any attempt at a second try. In addition to simply having impaired vision and hearing, it is clear that the tactile sense is also affected and the child is referred to as being 'tactile defensive'. Rather than having a dual sensory impairment, he is now truly identified as having a multi-sensory impairment.

Tip! Multi-sensory impairment can affect any combination of the major senses. Vision and hearing, however, are usually always affected.

Spectacles and hearing aids

Like everyone else, children with profound and multiple learning difficulties may suffer from a range of visual and auditory impairments which may be rectified, partially or wholly, by the correct use of spectacles or hearing aids. It is possible for experienced audiologists or ophthalmologists to test the hearing and vision of even the most profoundly disabled children. Specialized techniques can assess even those who are not able, for any reason, to cooperate while others can be carried out while the child is under sedation.

There are many different forms of impairments to both vision and hearing, although not all of these will benefit from artificial aids. While two children, for example, may be diagnosed with a hearing impairment, one, who simply needs amplification, may be helped by the use of a hearing aid. This may not be as appropriate, however, for the second child who is unable to hear certain frequencies. (Being unable to hear certain frequencies can affect the child's ability to hear certain vowels or consonants and may lead to a difficulty understanding the spoken word. Consequently, problems with communication may ensue.) Similarly, spectacles can help the child with, for example, myopia (short-sightedness), but not the child who is cortically blind. In this case, while the child's eyes appear normal the brain is unable to interpret what is seen and spectacles will be of no value.

All too often people use the expressions 'He can hear when he wants to!' or 'There's no point putting her glasses on, she can't see anyway'. Children with profound and multiple learning difficulties and additional sensory impairments face many struggles in their effort to make sense of the world around them, and any aids to help them achieve this should be both welcomed and used. It goes without saying that spectacles should be cleaned regularly and hearing aid batteries and settings checked to ensure they can be used effectively!

Tip! Always encourage children with visual and / or auditory impairments to use spectacles and hearing aids. This will help them to make the most of any residual sight or hearing.

Self-stimulating behaviours

Imagine living in a world where your senses of vision, hearing and possibly touch are severely restricted. In addition, your life experiences are so limited and your recall so poor that you have little to think or reminisce about, and even less to ponder over. External and internal stimuli, therefore, will be at an absolute minimum. This, unfortunately, is the case for many children with severe and profound learning disabilities and additional multi-sensory impairments. Is there any wonder then, that with such a lack of stimuli, many of these children resort to self-stimulating behaviours? These behaviours can take on various forms, but perhaps the most well known of these is simply known as 'rocking'. Many of us will have seen images of children in less developed countries who sit, isolated, rocking backwards and forwards for many hours, while here in the UK even the most well-cared for child may rock in the absence of other stimuli. While distressing to watch, rocking, and other similar self-stimulating behaviours, harm neither the child nor those around him. The provision of alternative stimuli, provided by the one-to-one attention of an adult, a favourite toy or even by a stimulating environment such as a Sensory or White Room can, in many cases, help reduce self-stimulating behaviours. However, while these can provide short-term stimulation, it is common for the child to revert back once this is removed. Consequently, some children may continue this behaviour for many years, if not indefinitely, and providing that it does not cause any harm or that it is not merely a substitute for long periods of isolation or neglect, it should be accepted as the child's way of simply passing the time when other stimuli are not present.

> Tip! Most self-stimulating behaviours are harmless and simply a way of passing time. Always ensure, though, that they cause no harm to the child or to those around him.

Finally . . .

Children with profound and multiple learning difficulties face many challenges and those who work with them must be ready to help them to face up to, and work towards overcoming, these hurdles. Each child, with his own unique combination of learning, physical and sensory impairments will demand tolerance and patience as he strives to make the most of his abilities.

Despite the obvious limitations, each child will have his own unique personality. Just as in any other group of children, there will be those who persevere, those who want to please and those who are simply too laid back to care! It may take time to get to know the individual characteristics of each child, but once he has let you into his world you will begin to adjust your own way of thinking to take pleasure, as he does, in the simple everyday things in life which we, in our high-tech, high-speed world often overlook.

5 | Sharing information

Say oh wise man how have you come to such knowledge?
Because I was never ashamed to confess my ignorance and ask others.
  –Johann Gottfried Von Herder, German critic and poet (1744–1803).

The passing on, and sharing of, information is part of our lives. We talk about the day's events as we sit down to eat with our families or feed back newly acquired information with colleagues at work. Sharing information helps us to better understand the thoughts and feelings of those around us as well as helping us to adjust to new or different situations. We handle this sharing of information in different ways depending on what kind of information it is or who is around. In addition, we can also choose how much information to pass on, who to share it with and even when to do so. Most of us have been in the situation where we are 'bursting' to tell exciting news to all around us and we repeat it over and over again to anyone who will listen. Similarly, there will have been times when those same people have had to 'drag' information from us as, occasionally, we prefer to keep quiet rather than to share our news, thoughts or feelings.

Imagine, now, how you would feel if you were unable to communicate your exciting news or to share your achievements or your worries with others. Perhaps your foot hurts where you stubbed your toe last night and it is painful to stand, let alone walk. Maybe you are feeling very hot but can neither remove your jumper unassisted nor ask for help in a way that can be understood by those around you. Children with severe or profound learning disabilities often find it difficult, if not impossible, to relate information due to their inability to communicate. It is the responsibility of us then, as fully communicating adults, to convey information on their behalf and this chapter will look at some of the different ways that this can be done.

Preparing for school

Starting school is a big step in any child's life, and with the exception of those in a few less developed countries, or perhaps the most remote, outlying areas of the world, attending school is an important part of growing up. The age at which children start school, the length of the school day, the curriculum they follow and the facilities provided may differ from country to country, but essentially all attending will receive, at the very least, a basic education.

Currently in the United Kingdom those with a learning disability may attend school full-time from the age of 3, remaining in full-time education until they are 19. Most, like their mainstream counterparts, will return home at the end of the day, although some, for various reasons, will attend residential schools, returning home either each weekend or at the end of each term. The type and choice of school depends upon many factors including where the family lives, the child's condition, local policies and facilities and, unfortunately, funding. One thing is certain, however; the days when children with severe learning disabilities were labelled as 'uneducable' are, thankfully, long over and the education system continues to adapt to make learning more accessible for all children, whatever their disability.

Before we go any further, put yourself in the place of a learning-disabled child as he begins the process of preparing for his first day at school. The excitement and anticipation of shopping for and labelling clothes, shoes, schoolbags and other essentials may help prepare the non-disabled child, as well as his parents, for that first important day but may mean nothing to you. More than likely, you will be unable to understand the reasons for these activities or to anticipate that a big change is ahead. Consequently, your first day at school may come as a very big, and very unexpected, shock. You may be taken by your parents into a strange environment filled with people you do not know and perhaps left there for an hour, a morning or even a full day. This new place will, undoubtedly, be very different from your usual surroundings, where people both know and understand you. Your parents at home will, more than likely, be able to anticipate your needs, understand your limited attempts at communication and know your likes and dislikes. Perhaps, being the only child at home, you will be used to getting the attention of those around you; indeed you may expect that when you cry, shout or simply refuse to cooperate, your demands will be met. But now, here you are in this strange room with other children who also seek the attention of these unfamiliar adults. You may find that you have to share, take turns and be expected to do things that, up until now, were done for you. You will undoubtedly be confused as your whole routine changes and you are expected to conform to the rules and schedules of this strange and bewildering environment – and all without the help of those you have relied on for the whole of your short life.

So, what can be done to help ease the child with learning disabilities into this new way of life? Many special schools encourage parents to bring their child into school for increasing lengths of time, over a period of weeks or even months prior to him starting full-time education. Often, these introductory sessions are scheduled to coincide with an activity that the child will enjoy, such as music, sessions in the school's sensory room, or a structured play session. The parent will often stay with him, initially at least, before gradually withdrawing for increasing lengths of time. This serves several purposes. First, it provides security for the child who, despite being in an unfamiliar environment, can still rely on the presence of a familiar adult to guide him through new experiences and situations. Second, it allows the teacher to observe the way in which the child and the parent interact and to make mental or written notes to ensure that the transition from home to school is as easy as possible. Finally, as well as allowing all concerned to get to know each other, it allows for the formation of a trusting and supportive relationship between all adults involved in the care and education of the child. In the long term, this relationship will benefit everyone, but especially the child, as he begins this new and exciting phase in his life.

Tip! Starting school is a major event in any child's life. Not being able to understand what is happening, children with learning disabilities may benefit from a gradual, carefully planned introduction to help ease any uncertainties and fears.

Information from home

As we saw above, the exchange of information between parent and teacher is essential if the child with learning disabilities is to transfer from home to school with minimal disruption. For the teacher, one of the most successful ways of gathering information about a child is, as we saw above, through direct contact with the parent. But what if this is not possible? Perhaps the parents have other, younger, children at home, preventing them from attending school with their child, or perhaps some other family circumstances make the child's gradual introduction to the new school impossible. An information sheet, similar to that shown in Figure 5.1, can be an alternative way of providing essential details about a child.

The basic information this information sheet provides will not only allow an insight into the people, events and activities that are an important part of the child's life but can also be adapted to suit different situations. Those in residential schools or respite care environments, for example, may benefit from knowing details about the child's sleeping patterns or how he likes to spend the time between his evening meal and bath time. Similarly, those in establishments for teenage children may also benefit from knowing whether

All About Me!

My name is: ....

I live at home with: ....

My brothers and sisters (if any) are: (please include ages)

....

....

I have some pets at my house. They are:

....

These special people are important to me:

....

I communicate by: ....

When I am happy I: ....

When I am sad I: ....

My favourite activities are: ....

But I don't like: ....

I eat and drink using: ....

My favourite foods / drinks are: ....

But I really don't like: ....

Other things I would like you to know about me:

....

....

Figure 5.1 A simple information sheet can be used to provide basic information about the child. It can be adapted if necessary to meet individual requirements.

the child has any special hobbies or which television programmes he enjoys. Adapting this to suit both the child and the situation ensures that the transition between home and any other environment is as easy as possible for all concerned.

Information from other establishments

Just as the transfer from home to school needs careful planning, so does the transfer from one establishment to another. While information from home may still be needed, other information relating to the child's prior learning will also be necessary.

Barney, a 7-year-old boy with severe autism, transferred from a mainstream school to a special school and was placed in a class of similar-aged children. Despite following a similar curriculum and a similar daily timetable, there were many changes for Barney to contend with. At his old school, he was one of 32 children all demanding the attention of one teacher. He did, however, have his own part-time teaching assistant, who worked one-to-one with him each morning. However, since he was unable to participate in whole class activities without support he often spent the afternoon playing repetitively with the same box of toys. Before his transfer, his new teacher visited him at school where she was able to chat, albeit briefly, to the teaching assistant who regularly worked with him and knew him well. She was told what he was able to do, explaining that he could count from one to ten, write his name and read several key words from the school's reading scheme. She also found out about his interests; he liked playing computer games, enjoyed colouring simple pictures and was surprisingly good at completing 30-piece jigsaw puzzles. He could understand simple commands and requests although his verbal skills were restricted to only a few words, including 'yes', 'no' and an attempt at his name which came out simply as 'Ney'. It seemed a useful visit, especially when, just before she left his new teacher was given a complete file with all his work and assessment levels.

However, when Barney started his new school the following September, his teacher was surprised to find he was not able to do as much as she had expected. Even allowing time for him to adjust to his new environment he remained isolated and withdrawn. He seemed uninterested in any of his work, even those tasks that he had apparently enjoyed in the past. After several weeks, however, his teacher realized that he would only work when a member of staff sat next to him and assisted him through his work. He had become accustomed to the one-to-one support given to him in his previous school and was unable to work independently. Because he had no way of communicating his anxieties or explaining that he needed help, Barney was left confused and bewildered, uncertain of what to do and what was expected of him.

The story of Barney highlights the importance of obtaining accurate information. The information given to his new teacher prior to his transfer was accurate, but what she was not told was the way in which he worked. She had presumed that he was able to work unaided purely because she had no reason to think otherwise.

> Tip! Always ask questions and never make assumptions about a child's apparent abilities.

Information from medical sources

Children with learning disabilities spend many long hours undergoing assessment and attending check-ups for a wide range of different conditions. Frequent visits to hospitals, medical centres, clinics and GP surgeries will result in long and detailed medical records, much of which is neither relevant nor accessible to those outside the medical profession. Essential information can be found in the child's Statement of Special Educational Needs, although it is often only when the child starts school that the way in which his condition affects his learning can be accurately assessed.

Some aspects of a child's medical condition, however, can change as he grows and matures, and it is essential that this information is updated regularly. Here again, a good, well-established relationship between parents and the child's teacher can help to ensure that everyone is kept up-to-date about any changes.

Every three months, 9-year-old Toby attended routine check-ups at his local hospital. After each visit his mum would bring him into school and report back any test results or changes in medication. This enabled all those working with him to both anticipate and understand any changes in Toby's behaviour that might be caused by an increase in medication or any changes to his physical well-being. In addition, she was able to discuss how well Toby had coped that day with the procedures and tests that were an essential part of his ongoing assessment. A seemingly minor point, perhaps, but since these hospital visits frequently upset him, his behaviour for the rest of the day depended on how he had responded to the demands placed upon him during what was, to everyone else, simply a routine check-up.

> Tip! Even a simple, routine hospital check-up can upset a child for the rest of the day.

The passing on of this type of information, however, is not just a one-way process and sometimes the experience of the teacher can help identify conditions that may go unnoticed by even the most attentive parents.

Elsa, aged 5, suddenly started to have frequent, though short, absences, lasting approximately five to ten seconds, before she suddenly laughed and began to focus again upon her work. Initially, these were dismissed as being yet another change to her frequently changing and often erratic behaviour. However, as these incidences became more frequent, a log was kept of their time and duration. After several weeks, her parents were invited into school to discuss the problem and to determine whether or not it was also occurring at home. Her parents, it appeared, had noticed these absences and just put them down to daydreaming. However, armed with the log that had been kept at school, they made an appointment with their family doctor who arranged for further tests. Some months later, Elsa was diagnosed as suffering from a mild form of epilepsy and was prescribed medication that soon brought her condition under control.

> Tip! Keep a record of any change in behaviour – there is usually a reason for it!

What did you do at school today?

Every day, interested parents in homes all over the world ask this question as they attempt to find out what their child has done at school. Many will smile in exasperation as they are given the answer 'I played in the sand again' or, perhaps even more frustratingly, as he tells them he has done 'nothing' all day! After more questioning, though, it often turns out that the sand tray was brought out because it was yet another rainy playtime or that 'nothing' means that it had been another day without any unusual incidences or exciting changes to the timetable.

Parents of children with learning disabilities, however, will inevitably learn very little from their child about his day at school. Problems with communication or an inability to recall the day's events will prevent this information from being passed on and discussed. To keep the parents informed of the day's events and to allow them to talk about them with their children, many schools send home a daily diary. Such a diary can take many forms, the simplest of which is a small notebook or jotter that can be placed in the child's bag at the end of the school day. It does not take long to write a few lines highlighting a special achievement or an activity that the child particularly enjoyed. However, within a class of perhaps eight children, parents may want different types of information to be passed on and often parents of the most profoundly disabled children will require the most basic information. Perhaps the child is under the supervision of a dietician, for example, and the parents need to know not only what he has eaten, but also how much and when. Or maybe he has problems sleeping and a record needs to be kept detailing whether or not he has slept during the day. Other parents may be pleased to read that their child has finally succeeded in completing a long-practised task, managed to write his own name unaided or even made his own choice of what to eat at lunchtime.

> Tip! Expect young children with profound learning disabilities to doze frequently throughout the day or to take a mid-day nap until long after they have started school.

A home/school diary does not always have to take this form though, nor does it need to be written by an adult. As the following story reveals, since most schools now have at least one computer in each classroom, older children or those with less severe learning disabilities can be encouraged to write, or to help write, their own diary.

16-year-old Lucas was motivated by any activity involving a computer. He was encouraged to spend ten minutes at the end of each day writing a simple sentence detailing one achievement, feeling or event which had been particularly meaningful for him. After printing it off, he then placed it into a simple ring binder and packed it into his schoolbag to take home to mum and dad. This enabled him to practise a whole host of skills including letter recognition and spelling, reading, recall, attention and concentration, fine motor skills, organizational skills, cooperation with a member of staff and turn-taking as well, of course, as basic keyboard and computer skills.

Very individual and highly personalized diaries are ideal for informing parents and carers about a child's specific activities. However, in addition to these, some schools also produce a weekly newsletter to keep parents informed of more general events and activities. This newsletter, which is identical for each child, enables parents and carers to keep up to date with what is happening in the classroom. Here, information relating to the whole class can be passed on alongside reminders about forthcoming events or details about what the children as a group have been learning in, for example, geography or art. This newsletter can take many forms with emails, school websites and school blogs rapidly taking over from the traditional paper version.

The importance of parental contributions

Just as it is important to relay information about events at school to parents at home, it is equally important for information to be sent from home to school. Children with learning disabilities may be easily upset by small changes to daily routine that, for others, may be nothing more than a minor irritation or inconvenience, as the following scenario demonstrates.

> *Ryan, aged 8, came into school one morning crying and screaming, refusing to let anyone take off his coat. He kicked out at familiar members of staff as they tried to console him and ran around the classroom upturning chairs and sending equipment flying in all directions. After 20 minutes of mayhem his parents were contacted to determine whether they could shed light on the reason for this bizarre and unusual behaviour. The answer was simple; they had overslept. This common occurrence had, however, disrupted Ryan's early morning routine. His mum had quickly bathed, dressed and fed him, but in a hurry to catch the school bus, had not had time to clean his teeth. She had to carry him to the bus stop and hand him over to the bus escort, who was unable to placate him during the 25-minute journey to school. Once the reason was identified the problem was soon solved. The school nurse supplied a toothbrush and toothpaste and Ryan was helped to clean his teeth, after which he quickly settled and sat down to his work.*

In a situation such as this, a scribbled message in Ryan's home/school diary, a phone call to school or even a quick word with the bus escort would have enabled those working with him to understand the reason for his behaviour and to find ways of comforting him. This contact between home and school is perhaps more important if there are longer-term changes to the child's family life. A parent being ill, in hospital or working away from home, the family pet dying or a close relative moving out of the area can be difficult for any child to cope with, but those with learning disabilities may require extra support from all who come into contact with them.

Finally . . .

The sharing and passing on of information is essential for all those working with learning-disabled children. Unable to communicate their needs and anxieties or to relay exciting information, many learning-disabled children rely upon those around them to do this on their behalf. Whether this is done by the means outlined above, or whether it is done by another method, one thing is certain: it should always be done. Parents, carers, teachers and others involved in the education and development of children with learning disabilities must work together to determine a method that suits them all, since it requires the cooperation of all of them to be successful.

6 | The learning environment

*Success depends upon previous preparation and without such preparation there
is sure to be failure.*

—*Confucius (551–479 BCE)*

Whether we realize it or not, any location has the potential to become a learning environment. We can learn much from visits to the woods, the coast, a museum or a working farm, for example, and each time we return, we have the potential to learn even more as the seasons and conditions continue to change. However, while we can learn a great deal from these environments, we do not generally have the freedom to adapt them to meet our requirements. Fortunately, though, we have more flexibility in that most traditional of learning establishments – the classroom.

All children learn better when the learning environment is suited to their needs, and children with learning disabilities are no exception. For those with severe or profound learning disabilities, the appropriateness of their surroundings will make a considerable difference to their ability to focus, to concentrate and, ultimately, to learn. No two learning environments will ever be exactly the same and very few, if any, will ever be perfect, but with a little forethought almost any environment can be adapted to optimize the conditions that help ensure successful learning.

This chapter will consider the effect of the visual, auditory and physical environment on learning opportunities as well as looking at specialized environments such as sensory or white rooms. The child's own work area and the seating arrangements of both the child and the adult will also be explored.

The visual environment

Making adaptations to the visual environment is often necessary to help enable those with severe learning disabilities to make sense of their surroundings. Think back, first of all, to your own childhood. Can you remember the puzzles that required you to spot, say, five rabbits 'hidden' in a hand-drawn picture of woods or the countryside? Their outline may have been disguised in the grain of a tree trunk or among a bunch of spring flowers. You may have had to search for several minutes to find the rabbits, looking carefully and concentrating hard, persevering until they were all found. Now, think about the modern classrooms of today. Compared to those of many years ago, they are attractive, bright, and appealing. Mobiles hang from ceilings, walls are covered with busy displays and multicoloured equipment adorns the tops of furniture and cupboards. For the majority of children, this riot of colour and shape will inspire, arouse curiosity and promote learning, but for those with a learning disability it may be simply too confusing. They may have difficulty processing what they see and too much 'visual clutter' may actually prevent them from seeing anything of any value. Just as you, perhaps, found it difficult to make out the shapes of those rabbits, so the child with learning disabilities will find it difficult to distinguish between the essential and the purely decorative aspects of the classroom.

This does not mean, however, that the classroom cannot be attractive and cheerful. Displays of children's work can still provide a showcase for their achievements while colourful friezes can continue to brighten a dull corner, providing, of course, that they are carefully planned.

> Tip! Display pictures or pieces of work separately on a contrasting background, rather than overlapping them, to ensure that each piece is seen instead of being lost in an array of colour.

Brightly coloured and highly appealing toys and equipment, designed to attract the attention of children, are obviously essential to any learning environment and a classroom without these would be a very dull place indeed. However, it may be necessary to consider where these are placed to ensure that, while they remain readily accessible, they do not become a distraction to learning. Finally, and especially in special school classrooms which already contain a large amount of specialist equipment, general day-to-day clutter should be tidied away when no longer needed. Even the simplest things such as a bottle of squash or a packet of biscuits left on the side can become a distraction if they are not returned to the cupboard after use.

> Tip! Try to strike a balance between making the learning area bright and cheerful and creating an environment that is visually confusing for those who already struggle to make sense of their surroundings.

Lighting is obviously an important element of the visual environment, especially for those with visual impairments in addition to their learning disability. This may come from a natural source (such as daylight coming in through the window), an artificial source (such as a lamp or light) or a combination of both. Think, for example, how the natural light in your own home allows shapes, colours, objects and people to be easily seen, yet it may still be necessary to turn on a light or lamp when reading, sewing or performing intricate tasks. On top of this, everyone's requirements may be different with age, tiredness or even a simple headache leading each of us, perhaps, to require different lighting conditions to complete the same task.

Traditionally, many adults have considered that children with visual impairments are best positioned by the window where natural light can help illuminate their work. While this may be the answer for some children, natural light can be very unpredictable. As the sun moves across the sky, as the seasons change or as clouds come and go, covering the sun intermittently and erratically, the availability of natural light fluctuates and, as such, becomes unreliable. In addition, some children, especially those with physical disabilities, may be unable to move away from bright light or turn their head to prevent it from shining in their eyes. Others may be photophobic (sensitive to light) or may be affected by the glare that bounces off shiny or reflective surfaces. While there is no magic switch to adjust the level of light entering the classroom, blinds or curtains can help cut down levels of excessive light. Unfortunately though, these may also have the additional effect of blocking out some of the light upon which the child relies.

Artificial light, if used, is obviously more predictable. Whether this source is from a central overhead light, wall-mounted lights, an angled table lamp or a clip-on lamp, the quality of light remains consistent. However, some forms of artificial light can cast shadows onto the very area you are trying to illuminate; a problem that can be increased if the child you are working with is constantly on the wriggle!

> Tip! Take care when using lamps to illuminate a work area. Trailing leads are a safety hazard and some bulbs, especially halogen bulbs, can become dangerously hot in use.

Advice on the most appropriate form of lighting for the child you are working with can be obtained from either the child's own specialist or a teacher for the visually impaired. More general advice can also be sought from the Royal National Institute for the Blind either online or via their telephone helpline. (See www.rnib.org.uk for full details.)

Tip! Different visual impairments may require different lighting conditions. Always seek advice on the best type of lighting for the child you are working with.

The auditory environment

Consider a close friend telling you a piece of important information or the latest bit of gossip while you are sitting in the quiet seclusion of a local park. Here, you are able to give your full attention to what you are being told and there are few, if any, distractions. Now imagine that same conversation in a lively, crowded pub. In such a noisy setting, the result is very different. Not only will you struggle to hear what is being said but you may also have to rely on other skills to support your understanding. You will concentrate on watching the mouth of the speaker and you may need to pick up additional clues from gestures or facial expressions. You will undoubtedly have to ask for clarification or for certain parts of the conversation to be repeated. You will do your utmost in fact, to make sure you not only get the gist of what is being said, but also that you have correctly heard every last detail.

Now transfer this scenario to the classroom. The days when children were expected to work individually and silently at their own desks are, fortunately, long gone. Instead, they are actively encouraged to work together for much of the day, to learn alongside and from each other, to discuss tasks and to find solutions to problems. Even with the rare luxury of one-to-one teaching, learning-disabled children may struggle to make sense of what is being said. They may have to contend with the noises of other children chatting and moving around the classroom as they collect resources and equipment. Cupboard doors may be slammed, equipment may be dropped or knocked over, chairs may be scraped across wooden or tiled floors and furniture maybe rearranged so that friends can sit together.

Tip! Try putting rubber feet on tables and chairs to cut out some of the noise.

Other noises, not under the teacher's control, may add to this auditory mayhem. The gardener may be cutting the grass just outside the window, for example, or the class next door may be having their weekly music lesson.

> Tip! Try rearranging the timetable if possible, perhaps going to the hall for PE while the class next door has its music lesson.

Whereas the adult in the crowded pub was able to block out any extraneous noise in order to focus on the information being imparted, children with learning disabilities may not have the ability, nor the motivation, to do the same. On top of this they may be unable to interpret the gestures and facial expressions of the adult they are working with and have only a limited understanding of the task being presented to them. Finally, to complicate things further, they may have a hearing impairment, perhaps only mild to moderate, but one that has not yet been diagnosed. Is it any wonder they are not responding to the task?

> Tip! Remember that children with severe and profound learning disabilities may be unable to separate unwanted sounds from those they are struggling to hear.

Those within a special school setting may encounter additional auditory distractions to those found, say, in a mainstream classroom. To begin with, classes are much smaller with a maximum of perhaps ten children, usually in smaller classrooms. Many of the children may be non-verbal or may be unable to physically move around due to a physical disability and while some of the sounds will be similar to those encountered in mainstream classrooms, other noises may well come from different sources. There may be children in the group who cry, laugh or shout out at random, clap their hands or repeatedly bang equipment or fists on tables or worktops. These sounds are less easy to control, especially when the children have severe or profound learning disabilities and are less receptive to the requests, rhymes or gestures that many teachers use to silence their class.

> Tip! Try finding a quiet corner for one-to-one work. If nothing is available, make your own area using padded, portable, room dividers. These will also help reduce unwanted visual distractions.

Despite class numbers in special schools being much smaller than those in mainstream schools there are usually more adults, and so consequently, a higher adult to child ratio. In addition to classroom staff, the number of professionals involved in the education and care of these children often means that there is a constant stream of adults entering or leaving the classroom. Physiotherapists, occupational therapists, speech and language therapists, the school nurse and personal care assistants constantly seek access to the children, and many will start a discussion about what they need to do or what the child has just done. Children with hearing impairments in addition to severe or profound learning disabilities will soon become baffled by other voices and confusion will arise as they struggle to focus solely on the voice of the adult they are working with.

Tip! A simple 'Lesson in progress. Please enter quietly' on the classroom door may help stop chatter from other adults entering the classroom.

For those adults lucky enough to be educating the child in a home (or home-like) environment, however, many of these auditory distractions can be eliminated. Here it is easy to minimize unwanted sound; the television can be set to record rather than play, the washing machine stopped mid-cycle if need be and the mobile phone turned to silent. In addition, and in contrast to the less comfortable classroom environment, soft furnishings and carpeted floors can help to partially absorb or soften any superfluous sound.

Tip! Soft furnishings can help absorb sound as well as helping to prevent distress to hearing aid wearers from the discomfort caused by echoes in bare and sterile surroundings.

In an ideal world, all classrooms should mimic at least some of the conditions found in the home. Until then, the adult must eliminate extraneous noise in the best way possible, assessing and reassessing it on a frequent basis to provide the correct conditions for the children with whom they work.

The physical environment

A third area to take into consideration when thinking about the classroom or work area is the physical environment. Often this is one of the easier environments to control, as it is less dependent on external factors than the visual or auditory environments and any changes made may prove effective for many months.

Within a group of children of any age, there will inevitably be a variation in height, and as these children grow and mature this difference may become more noticeable. This does not normally present a problem unless one of the group is exceptionally tall or significantly smaller than the rest. However, within a class of perhaps ten children with severe or profound learning disabilities this variation will be much greater. In addition to the usual variation, some, for example children with Down's Syndrome, will generally be smaller in stature than the average child of the same age. The first priority, then, when assessing the physical environment, is to ensure that classroom furniture is the correct height for all children. Think for yourself how uncomfortable it is when you are required to sit on a chair of the wrong size for too long or to work at a table or desk that is either too high or too low. In most cases, it is obvious if a child is using a chair which is not the correct height or depth, and while a physiotherapist or occupational therapist will advise on correct seating for each individual, general guidelines suggest that he should be able to sit with his back straight and fully supported, knees bent at 90 degrees and with both feet flat on the floor.

Once the child's seating has been checked, table height may also need adjusting. In most cases, this may simply mean finding a table or desk at which the child can work comfortably. However, in some cases, children may work better if the work area is angled and, in this case, the angle of tilt will need assessing in addition to the height. Other children, perhaps those with physical disabilities who may change from chair to chair throughout the day, may require a rise and fall table which can be set to different heights to ensure that the work area is always suitable.

Having selected the correct furniture the adult must then consider how this is to be arranged. The current tendency to arrange children at tables grouped around the classroom (especially the mainstream classroom) invariably means that, at some times, some children will have their back to the teacher. While this will not cause a problem for most children, those with learning disabilities, who may have a short attention span and are already struggling to understand what is being taught, will simply 'switch off'. Instead, it is important that they sit in a position where they can see the adult at all times thereby increasing the chances of greater awareness and interest. Rearranging furniture into more practical positions may not look as aesthetically pleasing to some, and having tables and chairs of different heights, styles and perhaps colour, may not meet the requirements of those who seek perfection and order in their surroundings. However, the needs of the children must take priority and those who like consistency and coordination in their surroundings must put these values behind them for the benefit of all those within the group.

Tip! Make sure tables and chairs are the correct size for each child and that they are arranged so that children face towards, rather than away from, the teacher.

The environment must also be assessed from a safety aspect. Children with learning disabilities are not as aware of potential hazards as their mainstream peers, nor do they learn as quickly from their mistakes. As they move around the classroom, they may encounter many potential hazards. A number of children with severe or profound learning disabilities, while mobile, may have poor balance or an erratic way of walking. In addition, regardless of whether or not they have a visual impairment, some are not aware of their surroundings. They may not yet have learned to avoid obstacles, and some will not only walk into furniture but will literally walk over other, less mobile children who may be sitting or lying on the floor.

Other potential dangers come in many different guises. The special school classroom, for example, will not only contain the usual range of tables, chairs, cupboards and storage trolleys, but also a wide range of specialist equipment. This may include standing frames, outdoor and indoor wheelchairs or adapted buggies, wedges and rise and fall tables to name but a few. In many schools, most of this equipment needs to be readily accessible and, due to lack of space elsewhere, must be stored in the classroom. Imagine having to negotiate your way around all this equipment when you have a learning disability, possible impairment to your senses, poor coordination, difficulty in walking and an inability to make sense of your surroundings! Furniture and equipment, then, should be stored in such a way that there is a clear route around the classroom (or, for those being educated in the home, around the house), and this route should be kept as consistent as possible. Additionally, obvious hazards such as trailing wires, exposed sockets, sharp corners on furniture (especially important if these are at head height), or doors which may trap fingers or lead out on to a busy street should be investigated and solutions to rectify these put in place. For those being educated in a home setting a range of further safety risks include gas controls on cookers, excessively hot water in bathroom or kitchen areas and unguarded stairs.

Tip! Think safety! Tables have sharp corners and are often at head height for small children, and a slammed door can seriously damage little fingers.

Finally, it is worth considering small changes to the physical environment that, while not essential, may simply help to make it more accessible.

Tip! Think about small changes. Door, drawer and cupboard handles can be changed to contrast with the background colour to help those with visual impairments. Small and fiddly handles can be swopped for ones that are easy to grasp to help those with poor motor skills. Labelling drawers with pictures or photographs in addition to words will help non-readers fetch and put away their own work or find their own equipment, thereby increasing independence while resisting the urge to change the classroom around simply for a change will develop familiarity and confidence.

Wherever the child is educated, it should be remembered that as the child grows or becomes more mobile the risks will change and the environment will need to be constantly monitored and assessed to ensure safety standards are consistently maintained.

Specialized teaching and learning environments

Specialized areas are often ideal learning environments since they have been designed with the needs of learning disabled children in mind. They seldom require any adaptations, although because of the uniqueness of those with severe and profound learning disabilities, some such areas may require minor or temporary changes to suit individual children.

The best-known of all specialized learning areas is perhaps the Snoezelen® (literally translated from the Dutch words 'snuffelen', meaning to seek out or explore and 'doezelen', to doze or to snooze). These rooms, also known as multi-sensory rooms, white rooms, or simply sensory rooms, combine fibre optic lights, bubble tubes, disco balls, infinity tunnels, wall projectors, twinkling walls or carpets and interactive switches with soft music and subtle fragrances to stimulate the senses. They are also used to promote early interaction and communication skills and to develop cause and effect (the knowledge and understanding that an action can make something happen).

Tip! Use a multi-sensory room to develop early interaction and communication skills through one-to-one massage. No special skills are needed, just soft music, scented oils and warm hands.

As with all specialist resources these areas are expensive to install, and while they are commonly found in many special schools and similar establishments, they are beyond the reach of many other learning places. However, while it is often possible to buy similar, individual pieces of equipment in the local high street or via the internet, these should be treated with the utmost care to ensure they are safe to use.

Tip! Remember that children with severe, profound or multiple disabilities do not understand the dangers of mouthing, licking or dribbling on to potentially dangerous electrical equipment or of the consequences of rough handling of equipment designed for decorative rather than educational use.

The list of other specialized learning environments continues to increase as society strives to meet the needs of children with learning disabilities. Hydrotherapy pools and spa pools, providing warm, relaxing environments, are particularly suited to children with physical disabilities in addition to their learning disability. ICT suites, fitted out with computers, touch screens, touch pads and switches provide a whole range of learning opportunities, from cause and effect to word processing skills. Soundproofed rooms are ideal for music therapy, while darkened rooms can be used to enhance visual skills. Soft play areas, sensory gardens, tactile corridors; the list is endless and even the smallest space can be transformed into a specialized learning environment with a little thought and imagination.

Individual work areas and positioning

The child's individual work area is, perhaps, the one learning environment over which the teacher has the most control. Here, the smallest changes can make a big difference. As the following story shows, even a simple piece of coloured paper, providing better contrast between work area and equipment, can make a difference.

4-year-old Josie came into school with severe learning disabilities and, despite no diagnosed impairments to either vision or hearing, she functioned as deaf-blind. She was able to sit unsupported and her fine motor skills were good. She showed no interest in either toys or, much to the dismay of her family, other people. She was motivated only by food and although she was not able to use a spoon she could finger feed with ease.

This interest in food was used as a starting point to develop Josie's visual skills. To begin with, red Smarties® were placed on a large sheet of off-white sugar paper in front of her, well within her limited visual field and within easy reaching distance. She soon learned that if she looked carefully, she would be rewarded with her favourite treat. This established, the Smarties were then placed in different positions, at random, on the paper. Again, it only took only a few weeks of regular practice for her to achieve this. She had now learned to use her vision to scan an area.

This was not the end of the task though. Gradually different coloured papers were introduced – yellow, green, blue, purple, orange and finally red. Although it took her a few months, Josie learned not only to use her vision to extend her visual field but also to concentrate and seek out red sweets on a red background – quite an achievement indeed!

The example shown above demonstrates how, by using and adapting an ordinary classroom table, a child can learn new skills. Had red Smarties been placed on a red table from the outset, Josie would have found it difficult to find them and even then, this might only have been a lucky coincidence. Similarly, if they had been placed on a brightly coloured, highly patterned plastic cloth, this onslaught of colour would have made the task confusing and, as a result, she would have struggled to complete her work.

> Tip! Use large sheets of coloured paper or plain fabrics to transform a child's work area. Pay particular attention to the choice of colour, though, if the child is, or is suspected of being, colour-blind.

Other ideas are just as simple. Using non-slip mats or clamps to secure equipment to a table will help prevent those with poor motor control from knocking their work to the floor, while trays with raised edges will keep all pieces of a puzzle together, preventing them from getting dropped or lost. Solutions such as these are often reusable, highly effective and inexpensive and, with a little forethought, can make a big difference to the child's ability to learn.

> Tip! Often, the simplest solutions can make the biggest difference to a child's work area.

When considering the child's work area it is also important that seating positions are considered. With no right or wrong place to sit, the adult must experiment to find the most appropriate working position for each child. Figure 6.1 shows three of the more common positions used when supporting children working at a table or desk.

Figure 6.1 Choose the best seating arrangement for the child you are working with.

In the first of these positions, the adult and child sit opposite each other. This position has two advantages. In the classroom, it ensures that the child can be fully supported through his work while still providing opportunities for eye contact and interaction. It is also useful in more social settings (such as at mealtimes) where opportunities for early communication can be optimized. There are some children, however, who prefer to sit and gaze into the eyes of an adult rather than paying attention to the task in hand. Here, sitting to one side of him reduces distraction and often provides better results. Where possible, it is usually advisable to sit by the child's dominant side. So, an adult working with a child who is right-handed would sit to his right, with the opposite being more suitable for children who are left-handed. The third position involves the adult sitting behind the child. This position enables them to work 'as one', using hand-over-hand techniques to complete a task or activity. However, it is advised that the child uses a chair with back support to prevent the possibility of inappropriate physical contact between adult and child or that this position only be used by parents with their own children.

Whole class teaching may also need to be reviewed. The traditional 'teacher at the front' approach will, more often than not, be inappropriate for those with severe, profound or multiple learning disabilities. Children seated around tables, possibly facing away from the teacher, or row upon row of chairs and desks or are far from ideal. However, by arranging the children (as well as teaching assistants and other support staff) into a semicircular or horseshoe arrangement, teaching can become more effective. With no obstacles to block or restrict vision, opportunities for eye contact and interaction are increased and those with sensory impairments can be positioned to make maximum use of any residual vision or hearing.

> Tip! Experiment to find the best teaching and learning positions and classroom arrangements for both the teacher and the child or children being taught.

Finally . . .

In the same way that a gardener prepares the ground before planting or a decorator prepares the walls before applying wallpaper, it is essential that all those working with learning disabled children properly prepare the learning environment to enable them to teach effectively.

However, because every learning environment is different, the list of adaptations in this chapter is by no means exhaustive. Each environment will present challenges that can, and frequently do, change at a moment's notice. It is our duty to adjust to these changes, adapting both our surroundings and our teaching style, in order to get the most from the children with whom we work.

7 | Language and communication

I think one's feelings waste themselves in words; they ought all to be distilled into actions which bring results.

—Florence Nightingale, British nurse (1820–1910)

Communication is an essential part of all our lives. It does not rely solely on the spoken word but takes many different forms. Whether we communicate verbally, via signs, through gestures, with pictures or through the written word, each of us has developed the skills necessary to successfully receive and pass on information. We communicate in different ways with different people and are continually refining and improving our skills. We look up unfamiliar words in dictionaries and learn new languages. We think about the way we use gestures and adapt this use so as not to offend those from other countries or cultures. Whether we realize it or not, we are all experts in the use of language as well as in the behaviours that enable us to communicate effectively with others. Even more impressive, we can perform these tasks instinctively, making us true masters of communication.

Language or communication?

All creatures communicate, a skill that is evident across the whole of mankind as well being innate in much of the animal world. A elephant cow, for example, will slap her ears against her head to call her calf or will interlink her trunk with another as a form of greeting, snakes may warn off intruders by hissing and peacocks will display their magnificent tail feathers in an attempt to attract the attention of the opposite sex. It is only man, however, who has gone beyond this, not only learning and perfecting skills in communication, but also mastering language skills in the form of the spoken, signed or written word.

The ability to communicate does not rely solely upon the use of language. A shrug of the shoulders, a disapproving look or a simple 'thumbs up' gesture are all easily understood forms of non-verbal communication. These same communication skills also allow us to interact, albeit simply, with people from other countries despite not being able to speak their language. Here, gesture, facial expression, pictures or diagrams, and even the use of simple, familiar objects enable us to make ourselves understood wherever we are. However, while a few words of a foreign language can increase understanding between ourselves and those whose native tongue is different from our own, it is surprising how few we need to make a difference. Those who have mastered even a simple 'hello', 'goodbye' and 'thank you' in the language of the country they are visiting will know that these few words alone can go a long way in helping to establish friendships and to develop relationships.

To be successful, any form of communication requires a minimum of two people, a 'speaker' and a 'listener' and the involvement of both is essential for it to be effective. The encouraging nod and smile given by a parent (the 'speaker') to an anxious or nervous child (the 'listener') motivates him to continue whatever he is attempting; a simple command and response without a word being spoken. Language, however, differs from other forms of communication in that it does not always require a listener. The person who talks out loud when nobody else is present is not communicating, merely using words and language either for their own sake or to express their thoughts out loud. Should another person approach, however, and begin to listen and respond, this then turns from a simple use of language into a two-way communication, or, as it better known, a conversation.

All forms of communication need to be of interest to both speaker and listener. How many times have you been 'talked at' by someone who, despite your obvious disinterest, continues to ramble on about a subject that, while close to their own heart, is of no interest to you? This can be common among some with learning disabilities, especially those with autistic spectrum disorders who, despite having learned to use language, are unable to read and interpret the basic body language, gestures and expressions of those to whom they are speaking. It can also apply, however, to the most intelligent of people; many of us will have sat through a speech or lecture where the speaker, despite knowing his or her facts, is unable to get these across in an interesting manner. The result is that while they continue to speak we, the listeners, simply 'switch off'. On the other hand, a different speaker, while putting across the same information, may be able to actively engage with the audience, hold their attention and keep their interest. It is possible, therefore, to communicate without the use of language, but to use language successfully we must also be able to use other basic skills of communication.

Tip! Next time you see a group of people chatting and interacting look out for non-verbal forms of communication. You will be surprised how much of this we use!

The development of communication in the non-disabled child

Before a child becomes fluent in using language he will have mastered many skills in social communication, preverbal and verbal communication. These skills run alongside, and intertwine with, each other and all are equally import-ant when mastering the complex process of communication and language development. The use of words, the ability to adjust tone of voice and volume or the ability to listen to, and understand, what others have to say are no more or less important than the ability to offer and maintain eye contact, or to use and understand body language, gesture, touch and facial expression.

The first communication between adult and child is a one-way process and occurs within minutes of a baby's birth. As the parents welcome their new-born child into the world, they talk to him, cuddle him, touch him, stroke him and hold his tiny hand and, alongside the process of bonding, the process of social communication begins. The first real act of two-way communication between adult and child follows soon afterwards. At only a few weeks of age, eye contact between the two begins to develop and a few weeks later the baby's first smile appears. Over the next days, weeks and months, and long before the acquisition of formal language skills, social interactions initiated by the adult will help build the foundations of communication and language. Turntaking, anticipation, body language, facial expression and gesture develop as those around the baby care for him, play with him and tend to his every need. Over the next few years, an understanding of personal space and appro-priate use of touch in communication add to this repertoire of skills.

Running parallel to these vitally important skills are the baby's attempts at vocal communication as well as his understanding of the spoken word. The first cries of a tiny baby, however, are initially based on survival instincts rather than intentional attempts at communication. He will cry because he is hungry, tired or uncomfortable and, to begin with, the adult must instinctively guess at the cause. It is not long, however, before the adult begins to distinguish between different cries and puts meaning to them. By 3 or 4 months the baby can laugh and chuckle and several weeks later he begins to use sound and intonation to attract attention. By 7 months he will have started to babble, being able to use both vowels and consonants to utter, among others, those first two long-awaited words: mama and dada. By 9 months he can copy sim-ple actions and sounds, while pointing and vocalisation to draw the attention of others to people, objects and events begins at approximately 10 months of age. The first real words are generally heard around the time of the first birth-day, by which time he is also able to understand simple instructions. From this point onwards, both expressive language skills (speaking) and receptive lan-guage skills (listening and understanding) progress in leaps and bounds until, by the time the child starts school at 4 or 5 years of age, his vocabulary consists of several thousand intelligible words, with 'baby words' having been dropped in favour of their proper equivalents. These words can be rearranged in different combinations, forming complete sentences that either offer information or ask questions and perhaps most impressively of all the child has mastered the complexities of syntax and grammar.

Most of the early communication and language skills mastered by non-disabled children are learned incidentally; they are not taught but acquired. Interaction between adult and child allows the developing infant to practise an array of important communication skills as well as how to influence the actions of others even before he has learned to speak. Imagine, for example, a baby sitting in his highchair while waiting for his dinner to arrive. Having learned that sitting here generally implies that food is on its way, he anticipates the imminent arrival of a welcome meal. If this takes longer than usual, he may attempt to attract the attention of the parent by banging the tray of the highchair, vocalising or even crying. The mother will respond by 'answering' her baby, often with a question such as 'Who's a hungry boy, then?' or 'Do you want your dinner?' While feeding him, she may continue to chat, making statements and asking questions even though, at this stage, she will not expect a reply. She may be rewarded, however, with eye contact, smiles and perhaps even vocalisations. New skills will develop at a rapid pace and soon the baby will be expressing likes and dislikes in the form of facial expression and gesture, or making requests for more by opening his mouth or perhaps reaching out for, and grabbing at, the spoon. This single activity, which will repeated several times each day, helps to develop and consolidate skills in preverbal communication and social interaction as well as, of course, the ability to taste, chew and swallow.

Now take this same situation a step further. Having been fed, the baby remains in his highchair while, perhaps, his parents enjoy their own meal. More than likely, he will be given a toy to play with, or perhaps a spoon and bowl to enable him to copy, practise and develop the skills required for self-feeding. After a few minutes, however, this may accidentally fall from his hand and drop to the floor. The parent will pick the object up and return it to him and, for the time being at least, this will be the end of the interaction. Some weeks later, though, he will begin to realize this can be turned into a game over which he can take control. Now, when he 'drops' the object, he will not only look to see where it has landed, but he may also look towards the parent, anticipating that it will be returned. As the object is retrieved and given back to him, the parent will, most likely, make some comment and he may reply by smiling, laughing or vocalising. Then the routine begins all over again . . . and again . . . and again! As well as understanding the concept of object permanence – 'Although I can't see it I know it's still there' – the baby has now learned how to initiate an activity. In addition, he is also perfecting skills in turntaking as well as continuing to refine other, previously acquired skills. Finally, and equally as important, he has learned that his own actions can influence the actions of others – and all without a word being spoken!

Tip! The development of object permanence ensures that a child understands that people or objects are still there even when they can't be seen.

Effects of a learning disability on communication and language

Children with learning disabilities can be affected by the same communication problems as their non-disabled peers. The causes are many and varied, and can be of physical, sensory, emotional and psychological origin or due to outside factors such as social deprivation. Some children may suffer from 'delayed development' where normal developmental patterns are followed but at a slower rate than usual or 'disordered development' in which development is both erratic and patchy. Others may have problems associated with speech (the production of sounds), or language (the understanding and use of words and sentences in both their verbal and written forms).

Tip! Remember that not all children with learning disabilities will suffer problems with language and communication.

Certain conditions, however, bring their own, unique communication difficulties. Abnormal development or physical abnormalities of the larynx among those with Cri-Du-Chat Syndrome, for example, will inevitably affect speech and language development while an inability to 'read' or understand non-verbal clues such as expressions, tone of voice or body language will affect children with autism. Some may simply lack the intellectual capacity to either use or understand language while others may have no or little interest in the activities of those around them and consequently no desire to communicate.

In addition to problems with speech and language, many with severe, profound or multiple learning disabilities may not learn the essential early skills that are a precursor to communication. They may be unable to form relationships with others, lack the ability to establish and sustain eye contact or be unaware, as mentioned earlier, of the effect of tone of voice or facial expression. Most non-disabled 2-year-olds, for example, will understand a sharp 'No!' accompanied by a disapproving look and, in most cases, will stop whatever they are doing. The child with a learning disability, however, may need additional prompts such as a sign, symbol or even physical encouragement to help him understand and to support the spoken word. Later, as he grows, an understanding of the rules of turntaking or personal space may be slow to develop, the latter of which can feel very intrusive to those in conversation with him. Some children may also lack the ability to understand the feelings of another person. Consider the following conversation between an 18-year-old boy with a moderate learning disability and a volunteer worker when they met, by chance, in a pizza restaurant close to the boy's home.

Elliott:	'Mr P, do you work at my Saturday Club anymore?'
Mr P:	'No, Elliott, I don't.'
Elliott:	'Why don't you come to my club anymore?'
Mr P:	'Because I moved away. I don't live here anymore. I am just visiting some friends today.'
Elliott:	'Do you go to a different club now then?'
Mr P:	'No, Elliott. I don't go to any club now.'
Elliott:	'Do you stay at home instead?'
Mr P:	'Yes, Elliott, I stay at home most of the time and read my books but sometimes I watch the football on television or I go out with my new friends.'
Elliott:	'Hmm, so you've finished working at my club now . . . '

(At this point he paused, deep in thought, before looking Mr P up and down, studying his obvious weight gain, and finishing the conversation with his final comment.)

'Well then, I think you should start playing football instead of just watching it!'

Elliott had mastered many skills of communication and language. His speech was clear and he was able to initiate and sustain a conversation, using language for a variety of reasons including asking questions and making comments. He could maintain eye contact, take turns at speaking and listening and his grammar could not be faulted. In addition, he was able to see that Mr P had gained weight since he finished volunteering a year previously and consequently offered a solution to what he identified as being a problem for him. What he was unable to do, however, was to understand the feelings of Mr P. Had this remark come from a non-disabled person of the same age it may have been regarded as tactless or insensitive and although in this instance Mr P laughed the comment off, it may have upset him had he been concerned about his obviously altered appearance. As far as Elliott was concerned, though, he simply stated what he saw and offered advice based on knowledge gained from his own family, personal experience or from the media.

> Tip! Children with learning disabilities often say things that others may regard as insensitive. They do not intend to offend and are often just expressing an opinion or simply saying what they see.

Children of all ages and abilities learn through repetition and those with a learning disability are no different. This is demonstrated by a typical greeting between Mahesh, a 15-year-old boy with severe learning difficulties and his teacher.

Teacher: 'Good morning, Mahesh.'
Mahesh: 'Good morning, Miss.'
Teacher: 'How are you today, Mahesh?'
Mahesh: 'I'm fine thank you. How are you?'
Teacher: 'I'm well, thanks. Come and sit down and start your work.'

There appears to be nothing wrong so far, with all the basic skills of communication and language being used appropriately. However, one wet morning the conversation took a different turn.

Teacher: 'Good morning, Mahesh.'
Mahesh: 'Good morning, Miss.'
Teacher: 'It's raining today, Mahesh. Did you get wet?'
Mahesh: 'I'm fine thank you. How are you?'

As we saw in the first example, Mahesh appeared to be able to hold a short, appropriate conversation with his teacher when he came into school each day. The second example, though, reveals that he did not properly understand the conversation nor was he using language correctly. He had learned that the same questions were asked in a set sequence and because of this was easily able to give the same set replies. However, when this differed he did not know how to respond and was unable to hold a meaningful conversation. His use of language was not as developed, then, as it initially seemed. Just as we are able to learn set responses to questions in a foreign language without really understanding what we are saying, so Mahesh had merely learned a set of routine responses to a familiar situation.

Echolalia, a verbal communication difficulty involving the repetition of previously heard words, phrases or sentences, can be present in both learning disabled and non-disabled children. It is, however, especially common among those with autism. It may take one of two forms, delayed or immediate. In the first of these, a child will repeat sentences or phrases, often in the same accent, with the same intonation and with the same level of feeling as they were heard, despite this being hours, days, weeks or even months previously. Often these utterances are used to convey feelings or requests ('Come on, let's set the table', for example, as a request for something to eat), although occasionally they can be repeated for no apparent reason. Immediate echolalia, the repetition of part or all of something just heard, can, however, be more frustrating for both the child and the carer. Questions with choices become a source of frustration as the real choice is obscured by the repetition of the last word or sentence.

Adam, age 7, suffered from immediate echolalia. Whenever he was asked a question, he simply repeated the last word he had heard. This caused many problems. He was given sausage rather than cheese pie for lunch, not because he preferred it, but because of the way in which the question was worded. Similarly, he was given orange juice rather than milk and an apple rather than a banana at break time. His frustration led to frequent temper outbursts. Eventually, it was realized that offering Adam a choice of real objects to accompany any verbal choices would help him make proper decisions. Now as well as the question 'Adam, do you want a banana or an apple?' he was shown both choices. Despite asking for the apple (the last word of the question) he reached out for, and took, the banana. His teacher reinforced this choice by commenting on his real preference, simply stating 'Ok Adam, you want the banana'. While this did not cure his echolalia it did enable him to make successful choices and, in doing so, reduced his frustration, behaviour and temper tantrums.

Tip! Make sure the child you are working with really does mean what he says and is not simply repeating the last word he heard.

So far we have looked at some of the problems associated with expressive language in those with severe or profound learning disabilities. However, as we learned earlier, receptive language is often affected by a learning disability. An inability to understand all or part of what is being said, whether it is spoken or signed, is common among those with a learning disability. Our eagerness to be understood, however, can sometimes make the situation worse.

Mrs W had spent twenty minutes playing with 10-year-old Zahra. At the end of the session she tried to encourage Zahra to help put away some of the toys they had been using.
'Zahra', she said, 'please help me put the toys away'.
Unable to understand the request, Zahra looked up at Mrs W and then carried on playing.
'Zahra, we need to tidy away now.'
Still no response. Undeterred, Mrs W tried a third time.
'Zahra', she pleaded, 'please help me put the toys back in the box'.
After several more unsuccessful and increasingly frustrating attempts Mrs W put the toys away herself.

Mrs W was not alone in this error; we all, on occasions, replace one command or request with another in an attempt to be understood. However, in this instance, Mrs W was simply confusing Zahra with too many demands and too much language. Perhaps she would have had more success if she had simplified her request and kept the wording consistent, repeating the same command until Zahra responded. It may also have helped if she had broken the task down 'Zahra, let's put teddy in the box' followed, when that was done, by 'Now let's put dolly in the box'. Additionally, she could have emphasized the key word in each sentence ('Let's put TEDDY in the box') or even paused momentarily after this same word ('Let's put TEDDY . . . in the box') to enable time for Zahra to take in and understand the instruction. To her credit though, notice how Mrs W used Zahra's name each time she spoke to her. By doing this, Mrs W. not only gained Zahra's attention but also ensured that Zahra was listening and focused before continuing with her instructions.

> Tip! Think about the way you talk to children with a learning disability and try to keep your wording consistent. Changing it may only add to any confusion.

Even as children grow and mature we need to keep our own language and wording clear and consistent when speaking to them. Non-disabled children soon learn the real meaning behind familiar phrases such as 'put your thinking cap on', 'pull yourself together' or even, in a social setting, 'on yer bike!' and they respond accordingly. However, some children with a learning disability, especially those with autism who may already struggle to understand the spoken word, may be bewildered by these strange and confusing messages. The request to 'pull your socks up', for example, may literally finding them bending down to do this, while the simple, everyday request to 'sit down' may find them sitting down exactly where they are! Rewording can avoid confusion; 'sit on your chair' is much clearer and less open to misinterpretation.

> Tip! Make sure your comments and instructions cannot be misinterpreted by those who take things literally.

Please and thank you

Children all over the world are brought up to be polite, courteous and respectful, and good manners are instilled into them from an early age. The appropriate use of 'please' and 'thank you' are often deemed as being the first step in this process and even as adults we continue to use them as a matter of course. There are times, however, when we, as educators, must question the relevance of these expressions.

Initially, all children will use single-word sentences to express their needs. As their language skills develop, they begin to string two or more words together, and sentences begin to take on more meaning. Most will pass through these stages with ease, picking up language by imitating those around them. A child speaking at the two-word level and who is able to say 'Daddy sit', 'Daddy gone' or 'Daddy car' is able to express much more than a child who can only utter 'Daddy'. The three-word level – 'Daddy car work', 'Daddy car home' or 'Daddy car shops' – extends this further. This is not the case, though, with 'please' and 'thank you' which offer little in additional information and are used purely to demonstrate good manners.

Habib started school when he was just 3 years of age. He was a chubby, sociable little boy who, struggling to communicate verbally, used Makaton as his main form of communication. His mum proudly told his teacher that he was able to make simple requests, being especially good at signing for food!

Each day, with his mid-morning drink, he was asked whether he wanted a biscuit or banana and each day, without fail, he would simply sign 'please'. When nothing was forthcoming he would repeat the sign several times waiting expectantly to be given something in return. His teacher was confused. Did his parents, both of African origin, use a different language at home or was his mum exaggerating his ability?

After contacting his parents, the answer was simple. Like most parents they had tried hard to encourage good manners from their son. When he signed for a biscuit they would ask 'What's that other word?' and only when he signed 'please' did he get what he wanted. Consequently, Habib came to associate the word 'please' with the reward. Still working at the one-word level and unable to string two words together, he used the one that, ultimately, brought him what he wanted.

Many children with severe and profound learning disabilities may have difficulty understanding and using any form of communication and many will struggle to progress past the single-word level. Is it necessary to insist that they add 'please' when they eventually succeed in making a choice or communicating a need? How much will they gain from learning to say, sign or use 'thank you'? With a limited understanding and vocabulary surely essential concepts such as 'drink', 'sleep' or 'mummy' are not only more important but also more relevant to their level of development?

> Tip! Do not insist on a child using 'please' until his language skills have reached the two-word level at least. And remember that 'thank you' is merely a nicety and, where a child is already struggling to communicate, other words may be more meaningful.

The role of the speech and language therapist

Children with severe or profound learning disabilities are frequently unable to communicate in the conventional manner. To the uninitiated adult, the lack of the spoken word implies that these children have no means of communicating. In reality, though, most are able to communicate in some way. It is the role of the speech and language therapist to work with each child, his teachers and his parents to assess and maximize the potential to communicate by whatever means are appropriate, including the use of both verbal and non-verbal means of communication.

Their role, however, does not end there. Many children with profound and multiple learning difficulties have problems eating and drinking orally and a speech and language therapist is able to assess and advise on feeding, chewing and swallowing, skills which most of us take for granted. In addition, they will work with those with physical disabilities such as a cleft palate or those who, despite being able to use and understand language, speak with a stammer or other speech impairment.

The majority of children with learning disabilities in special schools throughout the United Kingdom, as well as some in mainstream schools, will have access to a speech and language therapist as a part of their school curriculum should this be required, although the frequency of their therapy may vary according to need, time or funding.

> Tip! A qualified speech and language therapist can advise on all forms of verbal, non-verbal and pre-verbal communication as well as helping to develop eating and drinking skills.

Finally . . .

Communication is an important part of all our lives. We communicate in many different ways, with different people and in different circumstances. We adapt the way we communicate without thinking, automatically communicating differently with a 2-year-old child, a group of friends, with business colleagues or with strangers. We use communication to express our needs and desires, our likes and dislikes, to pass on and receive information, and to better understand the wishes and feelings of others. Without communication we feel lonely and isolated.

For many with a learning disability, learning to communicate and to use language, in whatever form is appropriate, is a difficult and complicated process. Communication, as we have seen, is not merely a matter of 'learning to talk', but the ability to use and understand all aspects of social communication.

8 | Augmentative and alternative communication

If a man's mouth were silent, then another part would speak.

—Arabian proverb

As we have already discovered in earlier chapters, the ability to communicate does not rely solely upon the ability to vocalize, utter words or master the complexity of grammar. Many children with severe, profound or multiple learning disabilities will never learn to speak, nor will they fully understand the spoken word.

Augmentative and alternative forms of communication, which complement, support or replace any attempts by the child to communicate verbally, allow even the most severely disabled child to interact with others, to express wishes and to make decisions. Some, as we shall see, rely on the use of gesture or signing, while others use technological aids. The most common forms of augmentative and alternative communication will be discussed in this chapter.

Gesture

Gesture is the simplest form of non-verbal communication. We all use it to various extents, regardless of our age or ability. Many people, often unknowingly, 'talk with their hands' and these natural gestures not only add meaning to speech but can be used to emphasis certain points or ideas. It is, in fact, difficult to talk without using some form of gesture.

Tip! Next time you have a conversation with a friend or colleague try sitting on your hands and you will realize just how much you rely on the use of your hands to support your speech.

Intentional use of gesture begins in infancy. A baby will raise his arms to be picked up, while a toddler will point to the cupboard where the biscuits are kept when he feels peckish. As adults, we put a finger to our lips to silence others or rub our tummy when we are hungry, and we respond to the gestures of others, either through our actions or via verbal responses. It would seem appropriate, then, to use an extension of this natural behaviour with children who are unable to speak or sign.

Imagine, if you can, a friend offering you a drink and something to eat when you call round to see her. Unfortunately, at the time of your visit a severe sore throat prevents you from speaking (although it's not bad enough to stop you from eating!). As you go into the kitchen together your friend asks whether you would like a chocolate biscuit or a cream cake to accompany your coffee. Unable to speak, you have several options. You could reach out and simply take the treat of your choice, but that might seem rather rude. You could shrug your shoulders as if to say that you don't mind, even though you quite fancy that gooey cake. Or maybe you could point towards your preferred treat. That wouldn't appear too rude and it would certainly make your desires known.

This method of communication, then, would seem an ideal choice for children with the severe, profound or multiple learning disabilities who are unable, for various reasons, to either speak or sign. However, pointing doesn't have to be done with a finger. In fact, very few of these children either understand the meaning of a pointed finger or have the fine motor skills to isolate their index finger and aim it towards an object. Those who lack the motor skills to move their limbs may simply turn their head and nod or even 'point' using their eyes. It is this last method, simply known as 'eye-pointing', which many children with profound and multiple learning difficulties are encouraged to use to indicate a choice or preference.

7-year-old Freya became an expert at communicating in this way. Unable to either speak or sign, with a profound and multiple learning difficulty and little control over her random and involuntary limb movements, she had no control over what happened to her. At breakfast, her mother chose her cereals and at lunchtime, while other children in her class were choosing between, for example, pasta or fish, a member of staff made the decision for her. Inevitably, there were times when they made the wrong choice and Freya refused to eat at all.

However, despite her limited understanding and poor physical skills, Freya was able to use her eyes well and was often seen looking at favourite objects. Eye-pointing, then, seemed the appropriate method of communication for her and, with the help of the speech and language therapist, a programme was developed using foods and toys that both interested and motivated her. It took many months for Freya to understand the task and to consistently make the correct choice. Her parents were encouraged to offer her choices at home and she slowly began to take more control over what was happening to her.

In a different class, 10-year-old Sam proved more of a challenge. Despite his severe learning disabilities and considerable physical impairments, he was extremely sociable and person-orientated, revelling in the attention of those around him to the exclusion of everything else. His eye-contact with people was faultless and his incredible smile attracted the attention of all, regardless of whether or not they knew him. Although, intellectually, he was much more able than Freya, the skill of eye-pointing took much longer to establish. Initially he was simply encouraged to focus upon an object which was of interest to him; a long and painstaking task which took him six months to achieve. His next step was to learn to transfer his gaze from one object to another; again a long and tenuous process which took almost a year to perfect. It was only when he was able to do this consistently, and without distraction, that the process of learning to use eye-pointing to make choices began.

Finally, a word on that 'grab' which we dismissed earlier as being rude and bad-mannered. Children with severe and profound learning difficulties who have no other means of communication may use this as their sole means of communication. Although to us, as fully functioning adults, this may seem unacceptable, it may be part of the learning process for children with no other forms of communication and an action that will, eventually, lead to other forms of communication.

> Tip! If a child understands the concept of making a choice as well as having the physical skills to reach out and grab, he will, more than likely, have the potential to develop other, more acceptable forms of communication as he grows and matures.

Makaton

Makaton is the most frequently used form of alternative communication among those with learning disabilities. Developed in the 1970s and named after the three people who developed it (**Ma**rgaret Walker, **Ka**thy Johnston and **Ton**y Cornforth), it is now used in over 40 countries worldwide. Makaton uses symbols, signs and speech to help people communicate. In the United Kingdom, Makaton uses signs from British Sign Language (BSL), while in other countries it is derived from the sign language of the local deaf community.

Makaton is much easier to learn, teach and use than BSL. In contrast to BSL, which has its own language structure, Makaton follows the same spoken word order and basic rules of grammar as the local language. It always accompanies normal speech rather than being a replacement for it. This allows the child to use both vision and hearing to make sense of what is being said, thereby increasing his chances of understanding.

Makaton consists of a *core vocabulary* of 450 words and a *resource vocabulary* containing over 11,000 words. Each sign is accompanied by a picture symbol in the form of a black-and-white line drawing that supports or replaces conventional text in the same way that signs assist in the understanding of the spoken word. The core vocabulary is broken down into eight stages with the most basic and frequently used signs (drink, thank you, mummy, daddy, etc.) being taught first. In practise, however, signs are often taught on a 'need to know' basis. This may result in some children learning signs from later stages before completing all the earlier ones. A child in a wheelchair making regular visits to the hospital, for example, may learn the signs 'doctor' and 'nurse' (stage 5) before 'stand' or 'sit' (stage 1). The topic-based resource vocabulary allows those using Makaton to extend their skills by adding signs and symbols appropriate to their age, circumstances and interests.

While normal speech and sentence structure are used alongside the signs, only the key words (main words) in each sentence are signed initially. As the child's understanding and signing skills increase further signs can be added to aid understanding. Consider the following sentence:

'Granny is going to the shops to buy some bread'

If only the three key words of this ten-word sentence were signed ('Granny', 'shops', 'bread'), these, along with situational clues (i.e., Granny putting on her coat, picking up her bag and going out of the door), would still make sense to most people. However, as the child progresses, other signs can be added to clarify it further. 'Granny', 'go' 'shops', 'buy', 'bread' makes it much clearer; after all, with just three signed words there was always the faint possibility that Granny was going to the shops to steal the bread!

It is not necessary, then, to know a vast array of signs to communicate. In the same way that a toddler can communicate using one-word sentences, those using Makaton are able to communicate using single-sign sentences.

10-year-old Anna was a prime example of this. Despite having no verbal language she was able to relate stories and events with considerable skill. She came into school one Monday morning full of excitement. The conversation between her and her teacher went as follows:

Teacher: Have you had a good weekend, Anna?
Anna: (signing throughout):   Auntie.
Teacher: Have you been to Auntie's house?
Anna: Yes.
Teacher: What did you do?
Anna: Party.
Teacher: Did Auntie have a party?
Anna: Birthday.
Teacher: Auntie had a birthday party?
Anna (nodding):   Cake.
Teacher: You had birthday cake. Was it nice?

Anna: Dog.
Teacher (puzzled):   The dog had cake too?
Anna: Me (mine).
Teacher: Oh dear, Anna, did the dog eat your cake?

At this point Anna burst into fits of giggles. Upon checking her diary later, it was true that she had been to Auntie's birthday party, and, yes, the dog had eaten Anna's cake when she wasn't looking. Anna, through her use of Makaton signing and a bit of verbal encouragement, had managed to retell the whole event without speaking a word.

Anna's fine motor and manipulative skills were good, enabling her to sign with accuracy and precision. This enabled her to be understood by all who had a basic knowledge of Makaton. However, this is not always the case and some, due to physical disabilities or other reasons, are only able to make approximations of signs.

8-year-old Aiden's general laid-back attitude and couldn't-care-less approach to life meant that he would never sign as accurately as other children and his mum frustratedly, but lovingly, referred to him as 'sloppy signer'. For a while, those around him tried in vain to encourage him to sign with greater accuracy, but to no avail. Eventually a decision had to be made: should his casual signing style be simply accepted or should his teachers and parents persevere in their quest for perfection? Certainly, a wider range of people would understand his communicative attempts more easily if his signing was done with greater accuracy. On the other hand, those who knew Aiden were able to interpret his signs, and therefore understand what he was trying to convey. Should those around him just accept his variation in signing, then, in the same way as they accept a variation in pronunciation? After all, could it not be argued that an individual interpretation of a sign is only the same as a variation in pronunciation due to a different regional accent? After much deliberation, the decision was made to accept Aiden's signing the way it was. Those who sign differently to others, for whatever reason, are still, ultimately, communicating, and it is better to accept this than insist on accuracy and discourage further attempts.

Occasionally, parents will ask whether the use of signing will prevent a child from speaking. Evidence, as well as personal experience, has proved that this is not the case and that rather than delaying speech, Makaton actually assists it. Those whose speech and language skills are simply slow to develop gradually drop the sign as the spoken word takes over, while those whose speech may never develop fully can communicate easily and effectively with those around them.

Having been used successfully in special schools throughout the United Kingdom for many years, Makaton is now used in an increasing number of mainstream schools, toddler groups and, thanks to the BBC programme 'Something Special', on children's television. The Makaton Charity (www. makaton.org) also works with police, supermarket staff, bus drivers and faith groups (among others) who are all keen to develop this skill, making it more accessible to an even wider range of users.

Objects of Reference

An *object of reference* is simply an object that represents an activity, place, person or event. Originally devised by Dr Jan van Dijk, for use with people who were deafblind, objects of reference are now widely used by children and adults with profound and multiple learning difficulties and make use of any functioning sense, or a combination of functioning senses. This makes them ideal for those who are unable to access any other means of communication or who do not respond to signs, symbols or photographs. By offering the object of reference to a child immediately before an activity, he can develop a greater understanding of what is about to happen, where he is going or who he is working with. Objects of reference can also be used to help children make choices, to help them develop a greater understanding of the environment and, in some cases, to serve as a bridge to more complex forms of communication.

So how do they work? Initially, an object is chosen which represents, say, an activity, ideally one that the child regularly enjoys. A cup, for example, exactly the same as the one used by the child, could be used to represent 'drink' while a fork or spoon could be the object of reference for 'dinner'. As the following example shows, in some cases different children may use different objects to represent the same activity.

> *Edward, aged 7, suffered from profound and multiple learning difficulties. One of his favourite activities was spending time in the school hydrotherapy pool where, with the help of a foam flotation aid, he could wriggle away to his heart's content, stretching and exercising his arms and legs and splashing all those around him. On the other hand, Mia, also 7, lay still and motionless (but totally relaxed) in the water, and needed to be fully supported by her teacher. For her, the best part of the activity was being snuggled up in a soft, fluffy pink towel before being dried, dressed and returned to the classroom. When choosing objects of reference for this activity, their teacher was faced with two choices; should she give them both the same object to make things easier for the staff or choose something that was meaningful for each individual? She chose, correctly, the second option and while Edward used a piece of foam cut from an old and well-used*

flotation aid, Mia used a small piece of fluffy pink towelling identical in colour and texture to that which was used to dry her.

The objects chosen to represent this activity were both suitable and appropriate to each child. They were the same colour and texture as the objects they represented, despite being smaller in size. However while these miniature versions of the real thing work well as objects of reference, miniature representations are not always appropriate. A toy car (representing the taxi ride home at the end of the day) or a plastic horse (the weekly Riding for the Disabled session), for example, bear no resemblance in either size, shape, texture or even smell to the real thing and many children with severe or profound learning disabilities will struggle to understand the connection between the two. It would be better instead to use something that relates to the activity, perhaps a seat belt clip or piece of seat belt webbing for the journey home or a section of a leather strap, identical to (or cut from) the reins, for the riding session.

While objects of reference can open up a new world of communication to those with a combination of multiple learning disabilities their introduction must be carefully planned. Each new object should only be introduced after the previous one has been successfully understood and should differ, as much as possible, in colour, texture and shape. Mia's parents, seeing her using objects of reference at school were determined to introduce them at home. In their enthusiasm, they unwittingly began to use a face cloth to represent bath time and it was several weeks before they realized how closely this resembled her object of reference for hydrotherapy. After discussions with her teacher, it was decided her parents should use a bar of highly scented soap, which, being the same as that used at bath-time, was not only more appropriate but also avoided confusion.

Picture Exchange Communication System

The Picture Exchange Communication System, known as PECS for short, was devised in the United States in 1985 by Andy Bondy and Lori Frost. Originally intended for use by children and adults with autism, it is now successfully used by people of all ages with a wide range of different conditions as well by those with communication difficulties. Aiming primarily to allow those with no recognizable form of communication to convey their needs and wants to other people without relying on speech, sign or gesture, PECS consists of six stages or 'phases'. As they progress through these phases, those using this highly structured system begin by learning to exchange a single picture in return for a desired object or activity. Once this has been achieved, picture discrimination, sentence building, replying to questions and making comments follows, along with the use of attributes such as shape, size and colour. Even those with severe and profound learning disabilities, many of whom communicate at the single-word level, are able to use PECS successfully as the following story reveals.

> *Maddy, aged 15, had a profound learning disability and no recognizable form of communication. Her vision and hearing were perfect and she was fully mobile. She displayed a range of challenging behaviours, the most frequent of which was hair-pulling. It was not uncommon to see members of staff literally on their knees on the floor after she dragged them, by their hair, to the ground; a behaviour that forced some female members of staff to have their hair cut short or wear a sports cap when working with her.*

> *After much discussion about the cause of these behaviours, it was noticed that they usually occurred mid morning, just before lunch and around three o'clock in the afternoon. It appeared, then, that hunger was the cause, but, with no identifiable communication, she demonstrated her hunger through aggression. Gesture, Makaton and Objects of Reference were considered since these were already in use in the school, but all were deemed inappropriate and, on the advice of the speech and language therapist, the Picture Exchange Communication System was started.*

> *Initially, Maddy was taught to offer a single picture (in this case, one of a chocolate bar) to her teacher and in return she was rewarded with the real object. Once this was well and truly established, a second picture was introduced, and Maddy learned that she could choose what she wanted to eat – a chocolate bar or a few crisps. Maddy's limited learning capacity meant that this was as far as she able to progress, despite attempts to take things further. However, even with just two 'words' her behaviour improved and her teachers could once again grow their hair and put their headgear back into storage.*

In an ideal world, Maddy would have carried the pictures with her at all times, making them available to her throughout the day. However, as Maddy's severe learning disability required her to have the pictures easily and visually accessible these methods were deemed inappropriate. Instead, her pictures were fastened to a board in the classroom using a small piece of Velcro®, enabling Maddy to simply pull them off as needed. Her parents, keen to continue this developing skill at home, kept identical pictures in the room where she spent most of her time, allowing her to use this system of communication for most of her waking hours.

Further information on PECS, as well as details regarding workshops and training provided by Pyramid Educational Consultants can be found at www.pecs.com.

Communication boards and books

Low-tech communication aids are classed as those that do not require batteries or electricity and, in addition to the methods outlined above, communication boards and books fall into this category. They can be used by children with varying levels of learning disabilities and can be as simple or as complex as required. When using communication boards and books, the teacher can make use of pictures, line drawings, photographs, symbols, words or even letters and numbers to meet the individual needs of the child.

Like all other forms of alternative communication, communication boards have the potential to allow the child to make choices and to offer information. Symbols or pictures can be accessed via any appropriate means including, but not restricted to, touch (using any part of the body), gesture, finger-pointing or eye-pointing. The size and shape of the boards, as well as the number of choices offered, can vary according to the child's needs and abilities (Figure 8.1).

Communication books, which are generally smaller and easier to transport, work on the same principles as communication boards. They are able to offer more symbols, resulting in a greater range of choices. However, their smaller size may restrict their use with certain groups of children (those who use eye-pointing to indicate choices or who have poor fine motor skills, for example). Symbol choices can be arranged according to subject (food, toys, home, feelings etc.) for ease of use, with the number of symbols per page varying according to the ability of the child. Both communication boards and communication books can offer a low-cost, easily adaptable way of

Figure 8.1 These two simple communication boards, both offering the same four choices, are laid out differently to suit different requirements.

allowing children with severe and profound learning disabilities to communicate their wishes.

Tip! Take care when using clear plastic to laminate symbols or when using clear plastic pockets for display purposes as occasionally these can reflect light. This glare can make it more difficult for those with certain visual impairments, which can, in turn lead to less successful attempts at communication.

Voice Output Communication Aids

Voice Output Communication Aids (VOCAs) are also known as Electronic Communication Aids or Speech Output Devices and, in contrast to the methods described previously, rely on battery or mains power to function. Most of us will have seen them being used at some time, often attached to a wheelchair and usually used by adults who are unable to communicate verbally due to a wide variety of medical conditions. They vary enormously in their complexity and have been specifically designed to promote communication, interaction, choice and decision-making.

Probably the simplest and best-known of these are the BIGmack and, more recently, the smaller LITTLEmack. These battery-operated 'buttons', available in a selection of bright, eye-catching colours, are lightweight, easy to use and easily transportable. When hit, struck or pressed, they allow short messages to be recorded and then played back and are large enough for those with poor motor control to use with ease. (The BIGmack is approximately 13 cm in diameter while the LITTLEmack has a diameter of 6.5 cm.)

15-year-old Nina, having previously learned to use a single BIGmack, had progressed to using two BIGmacks to help her make choices. Each one was topped with a photograph offering a choice of meal, drinks, musical instruments or activities, and she was able to both select and 'ask' for her preferred choice. She was also learning to use the Makaton symbols for 'yes' and 'no' to reply to simple questions and these, when secured to the top of her BIGmacks, not only allowed her to make her own decisions but also aided her learning by verbally reinforcing her choice.

While both BIGmacks and LITTLEmacks are commonplace in many special school classrooms, there are many other high-tech communication aids available. More complex communication aids, with either artificial (computer-generated) or pre-recorded voices, come in all shapes and sizes and can offer anything from a choice of three or four words to hundreds of words. They may use overlays to change the theme (leisure activities, colours, home, school etc.) or may add extra words by scrolling through different levels until the correct word is found. They can be operated by any controlled body movement including touch, head control, sucking, blowing or even simple eye movements and, if required, can be adapted for use with switches. Generally, however, the more advanced the communication aid, the less suitable it is for children with severe or profound learning disabilities. The advice of a qualified speech and language therapist should always be sought when determining the suitability of both high-tech and low-tech communication systems.

Total Communication

Total Communication is an approach based upon the combined use of many different types of communication. Gesture, touch, speech, signs, objects, pictures, words and symbols and high-tech communication aids can be combined to create a communication system relevant to the child. Such a system is entirely child-based and can be adapted to suit the needs and abilities of each individual. In addition, it allows for the freedom and the flexibility to change with the child as his communication skills develop.

Total Communication always begins with the child, focusing upon what he can do at any given moment rather than what he can be taught to do. In its most basic form, it relies on teachers, parents and carers interpreting and consistently responding to his facial expressions, vocalizations and gestures and giving meaning to their responses. (This is especially relevant when the child has profound and multiple learning difficulties and is unable to access other forms of communication.) Consequently, because every child is unique, each will have his own combination of communication types. It is possible, therefore, in a class of ten children, that each child will have his own mix of communication systems and the teacher will need to use, and respond to, ten different systems. Fortunately, this is not as daunting as it sounds, and, in the same way that we are able to respond to friends and relatives who use different combinations of speech, gesture, body language, touch and eye-contact, those working with children using Total Communication systems soon find this becomes second nature.

> Tip! Always seek the advice of a qualified speech and language therapist to help decide on the most appropriate form of communication for each child.

Finally . . .

With such a variety of augmentative and alternative communication techniques available it is obvious that every child can, and should, have the opportunity to communicate in one form or another. While the most commonly used systems are outlined in this chapter, it should be remembered that other, lesser-used forms exist and that a speech and language therapist will be able to provide further information on these if required. Whatever form of communication is used, though, whether a simple eye-point or a message conveyed with a high-tech communication device, no child, regardless of intellectual capacity, physical abilities or sensory function, should be denied this most basic human right: the right to communicate.

9 | Making the curriculum work

Those who wish to sing always find a song.

—Swedish proverb

Every activity has the potential to provide a whole array of learning opportunities. Whether these opportunities arise as part of a formal lesson or purely by chance makes no difference to the fact that we can use them to enhance our skills and knowledge in a wide range of subjects. Sometimes the knowledge we acquire will be used on a daily basis (such as learning to read or fasten our shoelaces) while on other occasions it may be 'tucked away' for use at a later date. We continue to learn throughout our entire lives, in a variety of settings and situations and through a range of different techniques and styles. This chapter will explore the way that even those with the most severe, profound and multiple learning disabilities can access a traditional school curriculum.

Incidental learning

Our thirst for knowledge begins at a very early age, and even the youngest child has the potential to learn from the simplest everyday activity. Long before they start school and, with it, their formal education, many will have learned to walk, talk, run and play. They will be able to count, to draw simple recognizable pictures and select their favourite sweets or snacks from the supermarket shelf simply by recognizing the colour and design of the wrapper. They will be able to differentiate between a dog and a cat (despite each having four legs, a tail, two ears on top of their head and each feeding from a bowl on the kitchen floor), a bus and a lorry or the sun and the moon. They will be able to dress and feed themselves, to understand the needs of others and will have mastered the basics of modern technology. Some of these skills will have been taught formally, often by the parent or carer and generally with the intent of teaching the child a specific concept or skill. Many others, however, will have been learned through a process known as 'incidental learning', or 'passive learning' where the child learns purely through observation, experimentation or repetition or as a result of pursuing other activities.

To consider an example of this, let us think about a non-disabled 3-year-old boy walking alongside his mum as they go to nursery school on a crisp October morning. The sun is shining, and the child walks through the fallen leaves that have collected by the side of the footpath. As he does so, the parent explains how, each autumn, leaves fall from the trees. The boy, however, learns much more than this, discovering that:

◆ at a certain time of year some trees lose their leaves while others may keep them
◆ autumn leaves turn from green to red, orange, yellow, gold or brown
◆ leaves come in a variety of shapes and sizes
◆ fallen leaves accumulate in piles by the side of the path
◆ when they are dry they are fun to walk in . . .
◆ and they make a lovely, crunchy sound . . .
◆ especially the big piles, which are much more fun than the little ones!
◆ but the wet leaves among them are not as exciting . . .
◆ and can be slippery.

And finally,

◆ just because the sun is shining doesn't mean it will feel hot.

And all this before even arriving at nursery school!

In the above example, the child learns, through a process of incidental learning, much more than he has been told. This knowledge will be retained and used over and over again in the following days and weeks. He will be able, too, to generalize and consolidate this knowledge, understanding that wherever he sees a similar pile of leaves, he can expect that the original activity can be repeated with similar results.

While many children with a learning disability are also able to acquire knowledge through this type of learning, their ability to do so will vary according to the extent of their disability, with the level of this ability reducing as the severity increases. They will undoubtedly need to repeat an activity many more times than their non-disabled peers. They may forget easily (but think about the excitement of 'discovering' something new each day!) or may be less able to generalize. Their ability to persist, to try and try again, and to overcome any additional physical or sensory problems will undoubtedly affect their success.

Tip! Never expect a child with learning disabilities to automatically learn without being taught. Incidental learning decreases as the severity of the disability increases.

Those working with learning disabled children need the ability to consider what a child can learn from an activity and then turn this around to be the main focus of their teaching. The 3-year-old in the example above may well have discovered for himself the qualities and features of the fallen leaves but those with a learning disability may need each aspect to be taught separately. A walk in the leaves, then, may be part of a maths lesson (size and shape), an English lesson (speaking and listening), an art lesson (colour), geography (seasons, weather, direction, following a route), science (properties of materials: wet and dry, texture), or even PE (walking and balance).

Lesson planning

Go into any mainstream school anywhere in the country and the majority of children will be learning similar things. Basic skills and knowledge in English, mathematics, science, technology, design, history, geography, art, music, religion and PE as well, perhaps, as a foreign language, are the basis of the curriculum in most state-run schools. Despite their learning disabilities, children with severe and profound learning difficulties will often be expected to participate in the full range of subjects, following a similar curriculum to that of their non-disabled peers.

Imagine first, though, trying to teach geography to a child who has no awareness of the environment beyond his own, immediate surroundings. Because of his condition, he will struggle to make sense of the most basic of modules. A topic on the seaside, for example, may mean nothing to a child living in the centre of a large city surrounded by tall buildings and fast-moving traffic. Despite our best efforts to try to replicate them, the smell and taste of the salty sea air, the feeling of cold seawater as it splashes on a child's feet and legs and the sound of gulls flying overhead bear little relation to sand or water play in a warm classroom. While activities to extend the module such as a tasting session with fish and chips, ice-cream or candyfloss or a Punch and Judy show can provide meaningful learning experiences in themselves, they will never replace the real-life excitement, nor the learning opportunities, provided by a day spent beside the sea.

> Tip! Remember that real experiences should be used whenever possible since these are much more meaningful than simulations in the classroom.

In addition to the consideration given to the appropriateness of the curriculum, those working in a special school must also consider the very individual aims of each student. Unlike a mainstream school, where the majority of children will have similar aims, each and every child in a special school class will have his own specific, and often very different, aims. Differentiation, or the process of tailoring each lesson to meet the needs of each and every child, allows the teacher to both maximize learning and to improve teaching at the same time.

> Tip! For differentiation to be effective the teacher requires a knowledge and understanding of the capabilities and limitations of each child in the class.

So, in what ways do lesson plans vary between the different types of schools? In the mainstream school, the lesson is planned to enrich a child's knowledge in a specific area, for example, science. However, in a special school, the teacher must plan to develop each child's individual and specific aims through a range of, in this case, scientific activities. The subject and lesson content is used purely as a tool to aid the development of other, seemingly unrelated areas. A science topic on electricity in a mainstream primary school, for example, may cover the use of electricity and electrical appliances in the home, the dangers of electricity, the use of batteries and the construction of simple circuits. This will be very different to the coverage of the same topic for similar-aged children in a special school, where those with severe, profound and multiple learning disabilities may struggle to use a simple on/off switch or may lack the fine motor skills needed to use a crocodile clip in an attempt to complete a simple circuit. Instead, the module may be used to develop early cause and effect responses through the use of simple switches and battery-operated toys, to build visual skills by teaching the child to respond to a flashing light, or, for the more able, to develop fine motor and pre-writing skills by having him use a glue stick to attach pictures of electrical appliances to paper. How much scientific language and content is used will depend upon the child's ability and understanding. Those using the glue stick to attach pictures to paper may cope with simple instructions or statements such as 'Let's find the picture of the fridge. The fridge uses electricity'. The child with the most profound disabilities, however, having located and fixated upon the light will need a simple, much-repeated phrase which may have nothing to do with the module being taught. Here a basic 'Good looking, Caitlin' or even 'Good boy, Jimmy!' may be more meaningful than words which fit the curriculum but mean nothing to the child involved.

> Tip! Even the most traditional curriculum can be used to develop essential skills and learning provided the teacher understands the capabilities and potential of each child.

History with a difference

As we saw in the example at the start of this chapter, unplanned and spontaneous activities can provide many opportunities for learning. Providing that those educating children with severe and profound learning disabilities can look beyond the obvious, these spur-of-the-moment activities can be just as beneficial as those that have been meticulously planned.

As part of their history curriculum, a class of 11 to 13-year-olds were required to study a module on local heroes, the focus of which was the legend of Robin Hood. Among these nine children was one boy who was unable to remain on his chair for longer than two minutes and a girl who, locked in her own little world, regularly refused to join the group, preferring to sit alone, staring into space and playing with the buttons on her cardigan. Few were able to recall what they had done at home the previous evening or even what they had eaten for lunch an hour earlier. The ninth class member, a boy named George, had severe and profound learning difficulties including severe developmental delay, physical disabilities and an almost complete visual and auditory loss. With the exception of this boy all had some speech, with the majority using single-word sentences to communicate.

The lesson began, each week, with an action song based on the tune of the traditional nursery song 'The farmer's in his den' in which the words were adapted to tell how Robin Hood lived with his friends in the woods. Each week, one child was chosen as 'Robin', and, while the song was being sung, he was encouraged to choose his 'Merry Men'. At the same time other children were encouraged to join in with the song to the best of their abilities. This activity, repeated in exactly the same way each week, helped fulfil the history aim of several students as, prompted by the song, they remembered from one week to the next what was expected of them.

The activities that followed this, however, were postponed one week when one of the children brought in a green felt hat and a toy bow and arrow set that her parents had bought in the Sherwood Forest gift shop the previous weekend. Abandoning all lesson plans, the activity that followed went like this:

The children all sat on their chairs in a circle while the child who brought in the hat tried it on. She was then shown how to hold the bow. A large mirror was held in front of her to enable her to see her reflection. She was encouraged to look at herself, to see the hat on her head and the bow in her hand and was told she looked just like Robin Hood. After much verbal and gestural reinforcement, she was then asked the question 'Who are you?' She duly replied 'Robin Hood'. Spurred on by this success, she was then encouraged to pass both the hat and bow to the child next to her and the activity was repeated. Eventually, the objects were passed to George, the only child in the group who was unable to either see his face in the mirror or understand what was happening. Instead he was encouraged to catch sight of, and fixate upon, the reflected sunlight that streamed in through the window and bounced off the strategically placed and angled mirror. The activity continued until the hat and bow were returned to the original child.

Tip! Songs and music are great motivators and can help develop memory and recall. Use them wherever possible.

This unplanned and spontaneous activity held the attention of all children, even the boy who was usually unable to stay on his chair and the girl who generally preferred to sit alone rather than joining in with everyone else. While it allowed the children an insight into how Robin Hood might have looked, albeit only for as long as the activity lasted, it also served as the tool which enabled each child to practise the individual and often unique aims which were common to every subject. Within this particular group of children some of these aims included:

◆ taking turns
◆ anticipation
◆ cooperation
◆ sharing
◆ concentration
◆ attention to task
◆ awareness of others
◆ interaction with adults
◆ interaction with other children
◆ receptive communication (listening and understanding)
◆ expressive communication (relating information)

- eye-contact
- visual skills – locating and fixating upon a light source
- recognition of self in mirror
- remaining seated
- fine motor skills
- gross motor skills
- understanding (of activity)
- memory and recall (and therefore history).

These aims are in no particular order and are by no means conclusive; a different group of children of similar age would undoubtedly have different aims. In addition, there may be several variations within any one aim. Some children, for example, may be required to sit on a chair without prompting or verbal reminders for, perhaps, one, three, or ten minutes, while others may need to sit next to an adult to achieve a similar aim.

> Tip! Remember – the aims of children with severe, profound or multiple learning disabilities often span the whole curriculum and are not subject-specific.

Prior to the introduction of the National Curriculum, teachers frequently abandoned their plans to concentrate on the interests of the children in the class. Objects found in the playground or souvenirs from holidays and days out formed the basis of many good lessons. However, with tighter controls on what is taught and more emphasis on meeting both individual and school targets, this spontaneity is increasingly becoming a thing of the past. The above example, however, shows the importance of following the lead and interests of the children. Good planning is obviously essential to enable children with severe and learning disabilities to make the most of their abilities. However, teachers should never be afraid to change plans at the last minute since these unplanned teaching sessions are often the most eagerly received by children of all ages.

> Tip! Don't be afraid to change your plans if an exciting alternative arises. Sometimes, a diversion can be just as meaningful.

Numeracy: making it all add up

In most special schools even children with the most profound learning disabilities are required to participate in the same range of subjects as their non-disabled peers and it is this group of children that test the ingenuity and creativity of the teacher the most. How do you teach children who have the most severe learning disabilities, possible visual and hearing impairments, physical disabilities and no conventional form of communication to count, measure or tell the time, all important requirements of their numeracy curriculum? How does a child who perhaps has no awareness of himself as a person learn to recognize numbers to ten or understand the difference between a circle and a square? While it would be easy to go through the motions of attempting to teach these what would be the benefit to the child? Would it not be better, as we said earlier, to use the subject (in this case, numeracy) as a tool to develop other, more basic skills?

Every morning Mrs M introduced the start of the daily numeracy session to a class of primary-aged children with severe and profound learning difficulties using a pot of children's bubbles and a battery-operated bubble wand. This activity always followed the same format and used, whenever possible, the same language. It began as a whole group activity as all adults recited a simple question and answer rhyme involving the days of the week. This then led to an individual session in which every child, in turn, was given the opportunity to help pop bubbles aimed in his direction. He was encouraged to watch the bubbles as they approached, reaching out and popping them (with help as required) and reacting to the feel of those he missed as they popped on his skin. At the same time, the adult working with him counted out loud as each bubble was successfully popped. At the end of the session, the child who had popped the most bubbles was declared the 'winner' and everyone clapped and cheered as his name was called out. It was discovered that within the group different children reacted differently to bubbles popping on different parts of their body. Some, for example, preferred them popping on their cheeks while others responded better when they popped on the side of their necks or on their arms. At times, the activity was doctored to give each child a fair chance of 'winning' or, on the advice of a visiting maths inspector, to experience, verbally at least, numbers up to, and including, ten.

Just as the 'hat and bow' activity above allowed the children to practise aims which were appropriate to their needs, this activity allowed each child to develop early skills essential for daily living, rather than focusing purely on mathematical aims. Once again, in no particular order, this group of children was developing:

◆ visual skills – eye contact with others / with bubbles
◆ visual skills – fixation
◆ visual skills – tracking (in different directions)
◆ tactile awareness
◆ auditory skills – listening to sounds and voices
◆ auditory skills – turning head to locate source of sound
◆ auditory skills – identifying familiar voices
◆ awareness of self
◆ awareness of body parts
◆ awareness of familiar adults within group
◆ anticipation
◆ cooperation with familiar adult
◆ taking turns
◆ fine motor skills
◆ gross motor skills
◆ visually directed reach
◆ bringing hands together in midline (if both hands used)
◆ allowing hands to cross mid-line
◆ possible isolation and use of index finger (a precursor to pointing)
◆ recognition of / response to own name
◆ question and answer situations
◆ expression of likes and dislikes
◆ requests for stop
◆ requests for more

And, just to satisfy the mathematicians reading this, the children were also experiencing:

◆ numbers up to ten, including zero
◆ sequencing (days of the week)
◆ shape (circular bubbles)
◆ quantity (amount of bubbles)
◆ size (large and small bubbles)

As before, this list applies to the children in this particular group and others may be experiencing or developing different aims. It shows, however, how simple, everyday activities and equipment can be used to stimulate and develop children with severe and profound learning difficulties.

Tip! Bubbles popping in a child's eyes can be both upsetting and painful. Children with profound learning disabilities may not understand that approaching bubbles may pop on their face, while those with the most severe physical impairments may be unable to turn their heads away. If in doubt aim the bubbles towards the lower part of the child's face or neck and ensure an adult sits close enough to the child to catch any stray or troublesome bubbles.

Spread the word, explain the reasons

The two activities mentioned above were, as we saw, used to fulfil aims and develop responses that appeared to have little in common with the subject being taught. It is essential that all adults working with children who have a learning disability understand not only what is being taught but also why and how it is taught. In the classroom, communication between staff ensures that those working closely with individual children know what is expected of each one and enables them to feed back the fleeting eye-contact, perhaps, or the attempts at sharing or taking turns which others in the group may miss.

However, it is also important to take the time to explain to parents exactly what their child is learning at school and why they are studying the subjects they do.

Annie, aged 6, had severe profound and multiple learning difficulties and was unable to sit without support, to speak, sign or vocalize, or to eat or drink orally. She responded only to the most familiar of voices or faces, showing her recognition of these by smiling broadly. Despite this, she studied the entire range of subjects that her non-disabled siblings studied in their mainstream schools. During one consultation evening with her father, her teacher discussed why Annie, too, had to adhere to a curriculum that seemed, in theory, inappropriate for her needs. Picking up the tactile (feely) storybook that Annie had taken home the previous weekend as part of her English homework, he learned how, in the classroom, she had been encouraged to distinguish between textures, to reach out and touch and to move her hand and fingers to experience them. At home, she also had the opportunity to practise auditory skills as the story was read to her, visual skills as she gave eye-contact to her Daddy and interpersonal skills as she cuddled up to him as he read to her. After thinking about what had been discussed, her father paused for a few seconds before saying 'Now I know why she does English!'

The father in this example was an intelligent man, yet, through no fault of his own, he had failed to understand the way in which the curriculum could be adapted to suit the needs of his severely disabled daughter. As educators, we should not presume that parents understand what we do or why we do it, nor should we rely on the annual written report to provide this information. Had he understood what was expected of his daughter, the activity would have become so much more than just a bedtime story and her homework would have taken on more meaning for both of them.

> Tip! Make sure everybody understands the aims of the activity as well as what is expected from each child.

Finally . . .

As we have seen in this chapter, even the simplest everyday activity can provide a wealth of learning experiences. From the 3-year-old walking in the leaves on his way to nursery school to the children studying Robin Hood as part of their history topic, each child was able, potentially, to learn so much more than it would appear at first glance. Learning does not always require expensive and sophisticated equipment; a glance around any environment will find toys and equipment that can be used to aid the acquisition and consolidation of both new and existing skills. Objects that appeal to the child will motivate and stimulate, and it is these that are the most effective learning resources, regardless of their cost. Always remember that what the child is able to learn or to achieve is much more important than what is being taught. Try to look beyond the obvious, be creative and, most of all, have fun!

10 | Learning through the senses

Use what talents you possess: the woods would be very silent if no birds sang there except those that sang best.

–Henry van Dyke, American author, educator, and clergyman (1852–1933)

All children are capable of learning new skills and making progress at a level appropriate to their abilities. However, those with profound and multiple learning difficulties will require time and patience as well as carefully planned and structured activities. Unable to learn through conventional teaching methods, they will rely on their senses to teach them about the world around them and to develop new skills and talents. They will have many hurdles to overcome before they can achieve even the simplest of tasks and learning will inevitably be slow. They will need to practise developing skills over and over again, all day and every day, and a consistent approach is essential if they are to succeed.

A sensory approach to the curriculum

Children with profound and multiple learning difficulties are, as we saw in Chapter 4, unique in their needs. They require a very different style of teaching to almost any other group of children. Tasks and activities must be broken down to their most basic elements, allowing the children's senses to play a significant and valuable part in the learning process.

To understand this further, let us look at a simple request from an adult to a child to 'Put your hat on'. Responding correctly to this simple request not only requires an understanding of the spoken word but also an ability to use up to three of the five major senses. The child must be able to either see the hat and to make sense of what he is seeing or to recognize it by touch, responding perhaps to the fabric or the shape or, more likely, to a distinguishing characteristic such as a pompom or peak. Similarly, and even before he has the ability to understand the spoken word, he must be able to hear different sounds and to distinguish between them. He must learn that some sounds can be combined to make words and that different words can be put together to mean different things. Depending on who is speaking, he may also be required to understand that the same word can sound different when spoken in a different accent or that the same words spoken in a softer, sharper or more urgent tone of voice may require different responses. To understand a simple command then, such as 'Put your hat on', the child not only needs to have a concept of 'hat' or 'on' but also needs to know that it should go on his head and not on, say, the chair or his knee. He must also be able, of course, to reach out and pick it up, know where to put it and be able to get it there. In addition to having the gross and fine motor skills to perform this task, he must, importantly, be able to use his vision, touch and hearing successfully and this is where all teaching should start.

> Tip! Before a child can learn anything else he needs to be able to use his senses; without this ability all other teaching will become irrelevant.

The term 'sensory curriculum' is used in many special schools to describe a curriculum that uses this approach. Many children with profound and multiple learning difficulties must be taught not only to use their senses, but also to learn through them. They must learn to use each sense in isolation as well as to use them simultaneously. Unlike their non-disabled peers, who automatically and unconsciously learn to look, listen, touch, taste and smell, many with profound and multiple learning difficulties need to be taught to use these apparently simple and basic skills.

Samir, aged 9, had a particularly profound learning disability as well as a physical disability that displayed itself in random, uncoordinated movements. He was profoundly deaf although tests to his eyes revealed that these were normal. Despite this he appeared not to see and while he appeared to look at objects placed in front of him, it seemed that his brain was not able to understand what he saw. Samir was, it appeared, looking but not seeing.

In contrast to Samir, Lucy, aged 12, had some functional vision although this was very restricted. She was able to see, and reach out for, shiny or reflective objects if these were positioned in the upper part of her visual field (i.e., at forehead height) and slightly to the right. Unlike Samir, she was able to use her limited vision and took delight in what she saw.

Both Samir and Lucy required work to further develop their visual skills but both needed a different approach. Samir, it appeared, needed to learn to use his vision from scratch, to be taught to look and to make sense of what he saw. Lucy, on the other hand, already able to make sense of what she saw, needed to work on the gradual extension of her visual field.

The above examples show the importance of knowing and understanding the true visual abilities of children with whom you are working. They both needed a curriculum that enabled them to make full use of any residual vision as well as to develop this further. An appropriate sensory curriculum running alongside the school curriculum was developed, allowing each (and others like them) to work alongside other children in their group while still following a specialized and individual curriculum of their own.

Make it meaningful

The pressure of the school curriculum can often result in children with profound and multiple learning difficulties passively participating in activities and tasks which mean little to them. In particular, the need to produce evidence of progress and achievement places pressure on teachers and other staff to provide an 'end result' or piece of work purely for this purpose. While head teachers, school governors and even parents may actively encourage this, teachers should consider how much value some of this has to the child's learning and development.

Several years ago a group of teachers attended a course to help increase awareness of the way that children with profound and multiple learning difficulties perceive the world and how much understanding they have of the tasks set for them. Working silently in groups of four every course member was issued with a pair of simi-specs, each mimicking a different visual condition, which added to their enforced auditory impairment. Each group was then issued with written instructions for the task ahead. Using any available functional vision, they were required to read these instructions and to complete the task within a set time. The teacher whose simi-specs allowed her to only distinguish between dark and light, rendering her virtually blind, had the most difficult task. With severely restricted vision and no auditory clues, she had little idea of what was happening and relied on the support of the other members to lead her through the activity. She was assisted in collecting resources, to cut, tear, stick and fasten, but despite all the tactile clues she remained unaware of what she was doing.

At the end of the allocated time the teachers were allowed to remove their simi-specs to reveal an 'end product'; a floral Mother's Day card made from shiny and reflective papers and brightly coloured beads and sequins, and finished off with a bright pink ribbon tied into a bow. Despite being able to draw upon memories and previous knowledge, the temporary lack of hearing and enforced visual loss had prevented three of the four teachers from each group from understanding either what they were doing or why they were doing it. Those with the most severe visual loss were the least aware of what they had done.

In many special schools, this type of activity is often repeated on a daily basis and the resources used in the activity described above can be found in most classrooms. Using hand-over-hand techniques, children are guided into producing artwork, cards or evidence of their studies. The Mother's Day card produced in the activity outlined above might have provided greater learning opportunities had other senses been involved. Instead of guiding a child's hand and helping him to hold a glue stick consider how much more meaningful it would have been if glue was placed on to a large sheet of card and the child was able to spread this using his hand. Similarly, instead of using shiny and reflective papers to make a flower, how about highly scented (and freshly opened) pot pourri? Now instead of using just vision and hearing, the child has also used his senses of touch and smell. Extending this further, consider the contrasting textures of the cold, slimy glue with the hard, dry pot pourri and then mix the two for a third and completely different tactile experience. While the child may not be aware of the finished result, he has been encouraged to use four of the five major senses and has contributed much more to the card than he would have done using only his sight and vision. Mum now has a card that he has actively helped to make. It may not look as tidy and it may have a few raggy edges, but instead of being the work of an adult assisted by a child it has become the work of a child assisted by an adult. And Mum really will be proud of it!

Tip! Think of the ways in which vision, hearing, touch, smell and taste can be used to make activities more meaningful for the child.

Little things mean a lot

Those working with, or caring for, children with the most profound and multiple learning difficulties soon learn that progress will be slow. It may take weeks, months, or in the most severe cases, years for a child to show a response to a person, activity or event.

Lottie, aged 7, had been in school since she was 3 years old. She had profound and multiple learning difficulties and severe physical disabilities. Her visual impairment allowed her to see only the brightest lights shining in a darkened room. She was able to hear well and was working on using this skill to recognize familiar voices. After four years in school, often working with the same few, familiar staff, she began to respond intermittently as they spoke to her. This continued over a period of many months until one Monday morning, as she was brought into the classroom, she smiled broadly in response to the 'Hello, Lottie' greeting of her teacher. It didn't stop there, though, and Lottie smiled each morning for a whole week. This achievement was recognized in the daily 'Good Work' element of the school assembly where she was praised for her achievement. Whether or not she was aware of her achievement is uncertain, although she did enjoy the attention bestowed on her during her moment of glory.

At first glance, Lottie's story showed that she was able to recognize, and respond to, a familiar voice each morning for one whole week. More than this, however, she demonstrated an enjoyment of hearing the voices of people she both recognized and enjoyed being with. She may also have recognized the classroom environment (although may probably not have understood that she was 'at school') and her smile was her way of saying that she was happy to be there. Her response was the equivalent, then, of a non-disabled child approaching his teacher and offering a cheery 'Good Morning, Miss!'

This simple response, one that we take for granted from other, non-disabled children, took Lottie a long time to achieve. Her disabilities meant that she was never going to learn to read or write, to learn how to add, subtract or multiply, or even hold a simple conversation with her friends. What she had learned instead was to use her hearing and understanding to recognize familiar voices and respond to them, a major achievement given her profound disabilities. All around her acknowledged this and were proud of her success. None more so, perhaps, than her younger brother, who, upon her seeing her 'Good Work' sticker, proudly went up to her, cuddled her and said 'Cor, well done Lottie, you've been really clever at school!' Then, turning to his mum he added 'but I wish I could get a sticker just for smiling!'.

> Tip! Never underestimate the importance and value of even the smallest achievement.

One task at a time

Children with profound and multiple learning difficulties often require input, as we have seen, from a wide range of different professional staff. The class teacher will aim to develop learning and understanding, the physiotherapist and occupational therapist will work on gross and fine motor skills respectively, while the speech and language therapist may suggest activities to develop early or preverbal communication. In addition, visiting teachers for those with visual or auditory impairments may also recommend activities to be practised on a regular basis. In most cases it is the responsibility of the teacher to ensure that all these elements are integrated into a suitable and relevant curriculum for each child.

Just as we need to concentrate fully when learning a new task, so do children with profound and multiple learning difficulties. Imagine how you would feel if somebody asked you to walk from one end of a balance beam to the other. Most people would struggle to maintain their balance and reach the other end without falling or stumbling. But now think how much harder it would be if, while practising your walking, you also had to take beads from a bag hanging from your arm and thread these on to a string. Perhaps you would fall off the balance beam as you tried to focus on the threading or maybe you would send the beads scattering across the floor as you tried to maintain your balance? More than likely, though, you would do both, resulting in neither task being successful. Yet similar demands are often placed on children with profound learning disabilities. In their best interests, and on the advice of their physiotherapists, they are taken out of their wheelchairs and encouraged to sit on sturdy and stable wooden boxes or seats to encourage upper body stability, balance and sitting skills (often referred to as 'box-sitting'). At the same time, they may also be required to continue other essential areas of their learning, based on a curriculum appropriate to their needs. Perhaps they may be required to practise visual skills to track a favourite toy or piece of equipment and to reach out and grasp this before being encouraged to play with it. Twisting, turning, reaching and leaning will all be a part of this, as well, of course, as trying to maintain balance while working on their sitting skills. As we saw from the 'beam and bead' example earlier, expecting anyone to learn, let alone complete, too many tasks at the same time will inevitably end in their failure. In the same way as you may have found it easier to thread the beads after you had reached the far end of the balance beam, children with learning disabilities will find it easier to concentrate on one task before turning their attention to something different.

Tip! Don't expect children with profound and multiple learning difficulties to do much at one time. Even a simple task like learning to fixate upon or track an object can be difficult enough without the addition of other complications.

All together now?

Go into the majority of mainstream classrooms and all children will be working on similar things at the same time. An art lesson, started at two o'clock may be finished and tidied away by quarter past three and, in a class of 28 students, 28 pieces of art work will have been produced. This is not always the case, though, in a special school classroom. Children with profound and multiple difficulties do not, as we have seen, work in the same way as their non-disabled peers. They may be taken out of the classroom to work with the physiotherapist, they might be absent because of yet another hospital check-up or they could be sleeping off an epileptic seizure. Their shortened attention span may prevent them from completing an activity or they may be distracted by other stimuli over which the teacher has no control (for example, bright sunlight streaming into the room or the fire bell being repeatedly set off as it is repaired or serviced). Alternatively, they may become so engrossed in an activity that they become vocal and upset when it comes to an end.

7-year-old Joshua was a perfect example of this. He loved anything messy and would quite happily sit for 10 to 15 minutes spreading paint or glue on to paper. This activity, apart from being fun in itself, helped him develop a range of skills including tactile awareness, visual skills, hand–eye coordination, fine and gross motor skills, communication and cooperation. His uncoordinated movements, though, meant that whatever was on Joshua's table also got into his hair, over his clothes and on to anybody who sat next to him. In Joshua's case, it was not a case of finding time when he was ready and able to work, but finding enough time for him to enjoy and benefit from the activity. The 10 to 15 minutes Joshua spent working was nothing compared to the 20 or more minutes spent cleaning up afterwards, including a thorough all-over wash and complete change of clothes which, because of his physical disabilities, usually involved at least two members of staff.

Those working with children with the most profound learning disabilities, then, must learn to be flexible in their approach to timetabling and time management. They must learn to adapt to suit the needs and moods of not only individual children but also the whole group.

Tip! Try juggling the timetable to allow all children to enjoy, benefit from and complete their work at a time that is best suited to adults and children alike.

One teacher, one child

Think back to your own primary school and try to remember the classroom set-up. More than likely you, along with perhaps 30 other children, sat around tables or at desks, while the teacher taught from the front. You would have needed to look and listen, pay attention and concentrate. As you grew and changed schools you may also have been required to read from the board, from a screen or from textbooks, to make notes, or to search for information. You would certainly have needed the ability to plan ahead, be motivated and to be able to take control of your own learning. Finally, whether it was for your own satisfaction or to please others, you would have done your best to produce a piece of work which merited either verbal or written praise, a gold star or top grades in an examination.

Now imagine that you had the types of disabilities displayed by those with profound and multiple learning difficulties and ask yourself how much of this remains relevant. In all probability the answer will be very little. The traditional teaching and learning styles which most of us grew up with are not appropriate for children with such complex disabilities. The problems associated with poor visual, auditory and motor skills, as well as severe intellectual impairment are only some of the more obvious obstacles faced by these children. Lack of motivation, attention and concentration, an inability to comprehend a task (or the reasons for it), a lack of awareness of cause and effect or even an inability to relate to others (and hence the desire to please them) all call for a very different and distinctive way of teaching.

Any class of children with severe and profound learning difficulties will need a high adult to child ratio. Due to their unique and very individual learning disabilities, the ideal ratio for these children is one adult to each child. In reality, however, this is rarely possible with only those educated privately or at home being lucky enough to receive this amount of attention. The adult to child ratio will differ from one special school to the next, and generally any class with a ratio of one adult to two children is considered to be well-staffed. Does this mean, then, that without one-to-one teaching the children will have less opportunity to learn? In theory, it would certainly appear this way, but in practice this is not always the case. Despite their real age, many children with profound and multiple learning difficulties function at a much younger age, and, just like all young children, they may doze on and off throughout the day. In addition they may find even the simplest activity exhausting due to the amount of effort required to complete it and may simply 'switch off'. Think, for example, how difficult it is to work when you have a heavy cold. Your concentration will be the first thing to go and everything will seem more of a struggle. Now try to imagine the hurdles that these children have to overcome and that mere cold somehow fades into insignificance. For many, the constant and continuous attention and demands of an adult may be just too much to cope with.

Tip! Allow children with the most severe or profound learning disabilities time to rest and 'recharge their batteries' between activities and they will approach the next task with renewed energy.

Another point to consider is whether the same adult consistently works with the same child. Certainly any adult working closely with a child on a regular basis will certainly learn to recognize his strengths and weaknesses as well as his likes and dislikes. She will also learn to recognize the tiniest movements, the simplest attempts at communication or the smallest signs of progress and will be able to respond appropriately. Maybe the disabilities or behaviours are so severe that the child would benefit from the secure and close bond formed by a relationship with just one familiar worker? On the down side, though, what happens when this person is absent? Perhaps rotating staff may be the answer. This will allow the child to develop better interpersonal skills and enable him to benefit from the particular abilities of different adults. Unfortunately, there is no one answer to this and different children, as well as different circumstances, will demand different solutions.

Tip! Consider, if possible, whether the child would benefit from working with a variety of different adults or whether his particular needs would be best met by the close working relationship of just one familiar adult.

Finally . . .

Teaching children with profound and multiple learning difficulties will be, initially, a real challenge for those with little or no previous knowledge of their condition. Learning to teach through the senses will lead them to become creative in their thinking, especially if they are required to follow a subject-based curriculum similar to that found in mainstream schools. These children require that those working with them both change their outlook on life and reconsider their priorities. Their progress will be slow, sometimes frustratingly so, but their achievements, however small, will be a cause for real celebration.

11 | Breaking things down

Little by little, the bird builds its nest.

–Haitian proverb

Throughout our entire lives, we continue to learn new skills and to develop new abilities. Some of these we learn quickly, while others may take days, weeks or months to achieve. We actively set out to acquire some of these, making a conscious effort, for example, to learn how to drive a car or to speak a foreign language, while others may be learned passively and without intention. (Remember that little 3-year-old walking to nursery school in Chapter 9?) Each and every one of us has a different attitude to learning and while some are keen to learn, others show less interest. Whichever category we fall into, learning is easier if we are interested in the subject or activity, and, because we are all unique, what interests one person may not interest another. Nevertheless, most of us enjoy learning in one form or another and are justifiably proud of our achievements.

Children with a learning disability will inevitably take longer than their non-disabled peers to learn new skills. Those with severe or profound disabilities will almost certainly require a different approach to enable them to learn skills and this often involves breaking down tasks into smaller, more easily attainable steps and building upon these until the task is complete. There are many ways of doing this and some of these will be investigated in this chapter.

One step at a time

Almost all tasks can be broken down into smaller steps, although some are much easier to break down than others. The easiest tasks are often those that can be broken down into a clearly defined sequence and which can be easily repeated with many different children. The number of steps within any given task will depend not only on its complexity but also on the ability of the child.

Let us look first, though, at an example of the way one simple activity can be easily broken down into smaller steps to encourage successful learning.

As part of his maths curriculum, 10-year-old Marcus was required to complete an alternating sequence of two colours. His particular fondness for threading brightly coloured beads proved to be an ideal starting point for this task. His fine motor skills were good and he was easily able to thread beads on to semi-rigid plastic laces. He was also able to match, sort and name basic colours. However, he was unable to understand the concept of alternating colours, or 'taking turns' and simply threaded the beads at random. The task, it appeared, needed breaking down into smaller, more achievable steps.

1. *To begin with six red beads were placed into a red bowl and six blue beads put into a blue bowl. Marcus then helped his teacher to thread these by first passing her a red bead then a blue bead, on request, until the bowls were empty. The string of beads was then laid horizontally on the table with the first red bead lying to the left. His teacher then talked Marcus through the task, describing how they had 'taken turns' with the colours and encouraging him to point to each one in turn as she worked her way verbally through the sequence.*
2. *Next it was his turn. More beads were placed into the bowls and Marcus threaded the beads as his teacher guided him through the task. She used both verbal prompts (saying the colours) and gestural prompts (pointing to the beads) to ensure that Marcus was able to complete the task successfully. When he was finished, he laid his beads underneath those of his teacher so that they could be compared. This was repeated many times until Marcus was happy with the process.*
3. *The next step was to remove one of the prompts. (In Marcus's case this was the verbal prompt although other children may benefit more from leaving this and removing the gestural prompt.) Working only from a gestural prompt, Marcus took turns threading the colours until the sequence was complete.*
4. *Once Marcus was confident with this, the gestural prompt was removed and Marcus learned to complete the task unaided.*
5. *When Marcus had proved he was able to sequence red beads from a red bowl and blue beads from a blue bowl, the next step was introduced. Now, instead of placing the beads in the same coloured bowls, they were placed into two white bowls, forcing him to focus harder upon the bead colour. Again, to ensure that he did not fail, he was helped with the task until he was confident enough to complete it unaided.*
6. *Marcus had progressed a long way and was now ready for the final part of the task. All beads were placed in one white bowl and Marcus had to sort through them, distinguishing between the two colours before he could finally thread them in the correct order. Once again, he had his teacher's example to copy until he was confident enough to complete the task independently and without support.*

By breaking the task down into several smaller steps, Marcus was able to complete a task that had previously appeared too difficult for him. However, despite completing the original sequencing task, he then had to prove he was able to generalize this skill and perform it with any equipment, at any time, in any place and for any person. In the same way that Rosie and Archie in Chapter 2 needed to learn to generalize their colour matching and counting skills, Marcus had to prove that he could sequence colours by not only using red and blue beads, but by using beads, toy cars, bricks, coloured stickers etc. in a variety of different colour combinations before he could be fully accredited as being able to complete this skill unaided.

> Tip! Breaking down a task into smaller steps may make the teaching process slow and lengthy but this has to be compared with the length of time, the frustration and the boredom of pursuing a task that would otherwise prove too difficult.

There was one other aspect was an important factor in Marcus's success; consistency. Throughout the entire activity the teacher always ensured that:

◆ Marcus always used the same colour beads
◆ the pots were always placed in front of him with the pot containing the red beads to the left and the pot with the blue beads to the right
◆ the completed sequence was always laid left to right underneath these pots
◆ Marcus was always prompted to thread the red bead first and then to continue the sequence with blue, red, blue etc. until all the beads were used
◆ the same simple commands, instructions and gestures were used each time

This consistency was necessary to ensure that the task remained exactly the same each time it was attempted helping Marcus understand both the task as well as what was expected of him.

> Tip! While non-disabled children can cope with slight differences in the way a task is presented, changing any aspect will, in effect, be similar to presenting those with learning disabilities with a new and very different task.

Writing for a reason?

As we saw in the above example, the ability to break down a task is essential if learning disabled children are to succeed, and the greater the disability, the further back the steps must be taken. However, in a school setting, it is all too easy to skip some of these steps in order to provide the necessary evidence that children are working towards or achieving specific goals.

Little Adanya had severe learning disabilities, poor visual attention and no formal communication. Each morning she would come into school, and, after being helped out of her coat, was taken to her table to start work. It was expected that, at 8 years of age, she should be capable of writing her name and, consequently, she was given this task each day. Sitting reluctantly on her chair, she was assisted in tracing over her name using a standard school pencil. She showed no interest in the activity and gazed around as the adult next to her guided her hand, helping her to 'write' her name. On paper, it appeared she had completed her task, and, regardless of how it was done, the school had the evidence to prove it.

The main reason Adanya showed no interest in this task was that it was clearly beyond her capabilities. Had this been broken down, though, into smaller, achievable steps she would have had more chance of success. She would have gained more by using her fingers to draw patterns in sand, painting with a large stubby brush or scribbling on a large sheet of paper using a chunky crayon or bright (washable) felt pen. (Remember that Adanya had poor visual attention; the bright colours and different textures would have encouraged her to take a greater visual interest in her work.) Only later, once these had been achieved, could pencil control be developed, which, in turn, would lead to the skills she needed to write her own name.

Tip! Do not rush children into attempting tasks that are beyond their capabilities.

Easy as ABC?

While the breakdown of many skills and activities may follow a set order with little need for deviation, others have a greater scope for variation. While the actual breakdown of these is just as simple, their application may vary from one child to another.

Imagine, first, if you were asked to list the skills a child should have before he is able to read a book. Perhaps you might write that he must know his alphabet or must know how to read individual letters or words. You may take a step backwards from this and add that he should be able to see what he is reading or should be able to speak to enable him to read out loud. However, if the ability to read a book is broken down further than this, i.e., to the pre-reading stage, you will find that many skills are required before the child can even begin the long process of learning to read. Presuming he has full use of all senses, can speak, sign or verbalize and has the fine motor skills necessary to handle a book, the child must be able to:

◆ locate the book
◆ pick the book up
◆ show an interest in the book
◆ orientate the book correctly (hold it the correct way up)
◆ turn the pages singly
◆ turn the pages from front to back
◆ 'read' the page on the left before the page on the right
◆ know that pictures represent an object, activity, event or character . . .
◆ and be able to interpret and understand these
◆ distinguish between words and pictures . . .
◆ and find the words on the page
◆ know that words are read while pictures are discussed
◆ understand that words (in the English language) are read from left to right
◆ know that the first line of any text should be read first, followed by the second, third, fourth etc.

Non-disabled children will learn some of these skills incidentally as parents, carers, teachers or even older brothers and sisters sit and read to them. They will be encouraged, for example, to look towards the page on the left rather than that on the right and will listen, initially, as others talk about the pictures. They may even be encouraged to 'help me read' by following the words with their finger, thereby encouraging left-to-right movement as well as the knowledge to work through the text from the top line down. Children with a learning disability, though, will not develop these skills as readily and those working with them must develop the ability to think through the activity and break it down into smaller steps if child is to succeed.

Unlike the skills breakdown in the last section, though, those outlined above are not necessarily in sequential order. However, while those at the beginning are generally acquired before those towards the end, the order in which they are developed may vary from one child to the next. In addition, progression through the sequence may become more erratic and less predictable if a child has a learning disability. If he also has visual or auditory impairments or if he lacks the physical skills to actually hold a book and turn the pages, this list will not only become much longer but will also become more individual to that child.

> Tip! Bear in mind that not all tasks can be broken down and taught sequentially.

Backward chaining

The tasks we have considered so far have all been taught from the beginning with the next step being added once the previous one has been achieved. This process is known as forward chaining. A second technique, known as backward chaining, is the reverse of this and starts with the last step being taught first. The theory behind this is simple; rather than requiring help to finish a task, the child always completes (or is helped to complete) the last part of the task and in doing so is able to achieve a real feeling of success. To demonstrate this feeling, think how you feel when, after several minutes spent trying to open a jar or bottle, someone else takes it and opens it for you. While you, having unsuccessfully completed the early stages of the task, feel frustrated, inadequate and maybe a little annoyed, the other person, having completed the final step, revels in their success.

This method, however, is not suitable for all tasks and skills. Imagine trying to apply it to any of the skills discussed above and you will appreciate its limitations. It is particularly useful, though, for social or life skills such as dressing and undressing, tidying toys into a toy box or helping to lay the table ready for dinner. So how does it work? As in previous examples, a task is broken down into small steps but rather than starting at the beginning, the child learns the last step first. He then works backwards through the sequence until the whole task is complete.

To illustrate this let us look at an everyday example such as putting on a jumper. A breakdown of the task may look like this:

◆ pick up jumper
◆ identify the top and/or bottom
◆ place hand into bottom of jumper and gather up towards neck opening
◆ place over head
◆ place first arm in sleeve
◆ place second arm in sleeve
◆ pull down at front and back, adjusting as necessary

In a convention skills breakdown, the first step would be taught first and then additional steps added until all tasks have been mastered. However, with this method, the adult performs all steps except the last one, and it is this that the child learns first. Once achieved, he then works back through the skills, learning them in reverse order.

Not all people, though, will put on a jumper the same way. If you were to ask around, you might find that there are a variety of different techniques. It does not matter which method is used as long as the approach is consistent and all those involved in the care and education of the child use the same method to avoid confusion. Neither does it matter, initially, whether the jumper is put on back to front as this can be taught later. After all, if a child is able to put his jumper on when he is cold, this is more important than not being able to put it on at all. However, if this is a concern to the child (and autistic children in particular may insist on the picture, logo or design being in the correct place) this extra step may be inserted at a relevant point in the breakdown and taught as part of the whole task.

This system, as mentioned earlier, is particularly useful for life and social skills, and therefore very appropriate for those being educated in the home or other similar setting. However, there are no hard and fast rules for this and the best way to determine the most suitable technique is often through trial and error. Break down the task, try it out and then decide which method best fits the task in hand.

> Tip! While we expect older children to collect cutlery from the kitchen when helping to lay the table we will simply give a young child a spoon and show him where to put it. By doing this we are, in effect, teaching through backwards chaining without even thinking about it!

Finally . . .

The old adage that 'success breeds success' applies to all of us, regardless of our age or ability. A severe or profound learning disability will inevitably make progress slow but by breaking one task down into several smaller steps, frustration will be reduced and the child will have increased opportunity for success. The time spent doing this will be more than justified by the sense of achievement felt by the child and all those around him when that seemingly impossible task suddenly becomes a reality.

12 | ICT (Information and Communication Technology)

Tell me and I'll forget; show me and I may remember; involve me and I'll understand.

–Chinese proverb

Technology is all around us. We use it everyday, often without thinking. Its uses are wide and varied; we press a button and the microwave starts, heating up our lunch quickly, cleanly and effortlessly, or we depress a slider and our toast pops up, a few minutes later, browned to perfection. We use social networking sites to reconnect with friends we may not have seen since childhood, or we press a known sequence of numbers into a handset and somewhere, perhaps on the other side of the world, a telephone rings. We may not understand how these things work, but every day, as technology becomes more advanced and more widespread, our lives become quicker, easier and more enriched.

The rate at which technology is advancing means that children are now growing up surrounded by it, both at home and in school. Unlike many adults, they show no fear of it; the effects of pressing a wrong button or hitting a wrong key worries us far more than it ever concerns them. Children with learning disabilities are no different and although technology may be used for different reasons and in different ways, it enables children with even the most severe learning disabilities to realize skills and achievements that, without it, might be very difficult to acquire.

Switches

Children learn through play and interaction, and toys designed for infants and young children are packed with features to help this learning process. Go into any toy shop and there will be toys with buttons, switches, levers and knobs all designed to promote investigation. Press any of these buttons or flick any of the switches and you will be rewarded with a whole range of different sounds, flashing lights or moving pictures.

Now think back to your own childhood. The toys you played with will differ according to your age, but you will, undoubtedly, have spent many happy hours playing and, as a consequence, learning about the world around you. Now put yourself in the position of a child with severe or profound learning disabilities who, perhaps with no understanding of cause and effect or lacking the imagination or physical skills to play, will be denied the pleasure and learning that even the most simple toy can provide.

Switches, simple devices which, when activated, have the ability to control a toy or other piece of equipment, can help these children acquire some of the basic skills of childhood. There are switches for almost every situation and every child, with the choice of switch dependent upon the needs and abilities of each individual. Switches can take the form of pads, discs, domes, pull-cords or joysticks and can be touched, pressed, squeezed, pulled or moved. Others can be operated through sucking, blowing or sound (including tongue-clicking). They can be trodden on (as in pressure mats), vibrate when touched or activated by sensors responding to the smallest movement, including blinking, finger movements or facial twitches. They can be placed on the child's work area, clamped on to a wheelchair, attached to a strap and worn on the head or positioned under an elbow or chin. Metal, plastic, foam, fabric or fur switches or switches that are smooth, ridged or textured can provide tactile stimulation and reinforcement as well as catering for those who may be tactile defensive, while auditory feedback can be provided by switches that click when used (Figure 12.1). The possibilities are endless!

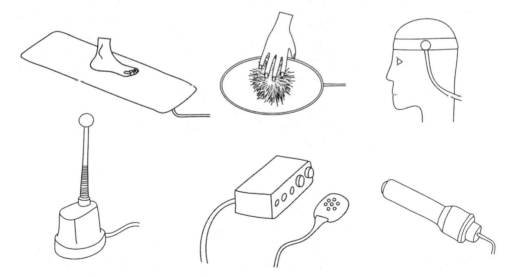

Figure 12.1   A few of the many switches currently on the market. Top row: Pressure Mat, Soft Koosh Switch, Tilt Switch. Bottom row: Wobble Switch, Sound Operated Switch, Grasp Switch (Switches not shown to scale)

Tip! Consider the child's intellectual, physical and sensory abilities when choosing the correct switch for him.

Switched toys (those that operate via a switch) are often used to develop cause and effect in children with severe or profound learning disabilities. These toys are widely available in specialist shops and on the internet. However, most battery-operated toys can be quickly and easily adapted for use with a switch by using a battery switch adaptor. Placed between the battery and its contact, this effectively breaks the circuit and allows a switch to take control. The following story shows how one boy learned to use a switch to operate such a toy, developing, as he did so, early cause and effect responses.

7-year-old Ewan had profound and multiple learning difficulties as well as a physical disability that resulted in poor motor co-ordination. He showed little interest in his surroundings, lacked motivation and had no real understanding of cause and effect. He did however, have a few favourite toys, the most loved of which was a fluffy, battery-operated pig that snuffled around his table top, grunting as it did so. Every time the pig approached him, Ewan would laugh, giggle and desperately try to reach out for it, struggling to coordinate his movements.

Ewan's love of this simple toy was used to help him develop his understanding of cause and effect. A simple plastic switch was fitted and, over time, he was encouraged to reach out and strike this, using, in his case, the palm of his hand. Eventually, as the months passed, Ewan learned that his action could cause an otherwise quiet and stationary pig to start grunting and moving. Now, rather than relying on an adult to operate the pig, Ewan was able to do it for himself and he was delighted with his achievements!

In the story above, as long as Ewan's hand maintained contact with the switch, the pig continued to snuffle, move and grunt. However, a control box (also known as a switch/latch timer) fitted between the toy and the switch can vary the way the switch is used. These usually have two settings, 'timed' and 'latched'. Setting this to 'timed' will activate the toy for specified lengths of time (usually between one second and one hour) while 'latched' will turn it on or off alternately every time the switch is used. These settings allow children to further develop their skills and are usually only recommended once cause and effect has been established.

> Tip! When using the timed function start with a setting of only a few seconds. Increase this only when the child's can maintain attention for longer periods of time.

The use of switches is not restricted to toys. They can also be used with mains-operated equipment such as fans, music systems or footspas. (There will be more about this later.) By carefully positioning a mains controller between the switch and a piece of electrical equipment children (especially older children) can learn to operate these themselves. It goes without saying, of course, that while such activities are generally safe, care must always be taken with mains-operated equipment to prevent injury to either the child or to those around him.

Computers, keyboards and mice

Computers are a part of our lives and, for many people they are an essential part of day-to-day living. They provide opportunities for learning as well as for leisure and are accessible by all, regardless of age or ability. Modifications to standard equipment can enable all children, even those with severe and profound learning disabilities, to use technology to enhance their learning.

Rosie, aged 11, loved using the computer, despite her moderate to severe learning disability, poor coordination and a considerable visual impairment. It motivated her more than any other activity and, at the same time, helped increase her attention, concentration, gross motor skills and visual awareness. To begin with Rosie used a switch to change the brightly coloured images on the screen in front of her. Over time, however, the activity was extended to encourage her to track moving objects as they crossed from left to right, and then at random, across the screen. Each time the object disappeared from view, she used the switch to start it up again and a different object would follow a different route. Her teacher could change the speed at which this travelled and frequently did so, especially if Rosie was having one of her 'off days'. This simple activity, which helped develop and extend Rosie's visual skills in a motivating and enjoyable way, also allowed her to practise her gross motor skills as well as to consolidate skills in cause and effect.

Patrick, also aged 11 and also with a visual impairment, used his computer very differently. Unable to grasp a pencil, and therefore unable to write his name on paper, he was learning, instead, to do this on a computer. However, his poor vision made it very difficult for him to find the letters on a conventional QWERTY keyboard. He was given, instead, an alphabetically arranged keyboard with large, brightly coloured and easily visible keys, making the letters much easier to find. Font size and style as well as background–letter contrast were adjusted to enable him to easily read the letters on screen. These simple adjustments were sufficient to allow Patrick to locate and identify the letters in his name, sequence them correctly and then to check them on the screen, skills that would have been impossible with ordinary equipment.

The modifications made to help Rosie and Patrick better use a computer are only some of the many ways in which computers can be made accessible. Keyboards, as we have seen, can be adapted to meet the needs of the individual. Big keys, high contrast keyboards, alternative layout, concept or overlay keyboards and ergonomic keyboards can replace the standard design, while vinyl character stickers in different fonts and colour combinations can cheaply and easily transform any keyboard. The conventional mouse can be replaced with a joystick or a rollerball mouse, perhaps with recessed or brightly coloured buttons for ease of use and accuracy as well as, of course, a whole range of different switches. Touch screens or interactive plasma screens eliminate the need for either a keyboard or a mouse, and allow the child to concentrate solely on the images on screen. Many of these screens are also height-adjustable and can be angled for maximum visibility.

> Tip! Make sure the computer screen is at the correct height and angle for the child to see it properly. Use a rise and fall table if necessary.

Prerequisites and precautions

The use of switches and computers can, as we have seen, be fundamental to learning. Their advantages are many and varied. However, as with all equipment and all activities, it is essential that they are used correctly with each child and the following points must be taken into consideration:

◆ Does the child know where the switch is? By always placing it in the same position (at least initially) he will learn exactly where to find it and any uncertainty is eliminated.

- ◆ Will the child knock it off? Children with uncontrolled or involuntary movements frequently knock equipment to the floor. The use of clamps, tapes or sticky adhesives can help to prevent this.
- ◆ Can the child use it easily? Do all aspects of the switch meet his needs, including, where necessary, the ability to release the switch as easily as the ability to grasp and activate it?
- ◆ Can the child transfer his gaze from the switch to the toy, screen or equipment being used?
- ◆ When switches are being used to develop cause and effect can you be sure that he is responding to the use of the switch rather than being attracted to the toy, screen, or equipment by the sounds, images or movement produced? (You will need to know the child and to be able to interpret his responses correctly to be sure of this.)

The use of computers, while essential for learning, may also need monitoring. Flashing lights and images on a computer screen can, in a small number of cases, bring on an epileptic seizure. While this is rare, children prone to these attacks should be carefully supervised to prevent this from happening.

Consider, now, the following story which demonstrates the potential risks of unrecognized computer abilities in autistic children with severe learning disabilities.

Aijay, aged 14 and diagnosed as severely autistic was, like many children of the same age, fascinated by the computer. His computer skills were good, he was able to use a conventional keyboard and he could perform many basic computer functions. When not spending time playing computer games, he could be found playing with his prized collection of toy fire engines.

One day, however, his father received an email from an online auction site congratulating him on his recent purchase and giving him instructions regarding payment. Confused, he questioned the transaction. After some time, and much thought, he was shocked to realize that his son had been the successful bidder. Having seen his father bid for items in the past, Aijay had carefully watched how it was done and, being aware that after bidding successfully, the goods arrived in the post a few days later, he had successfully bought another toy fire engine to add to his already vast collection.

Unaware that Aijay had the skills to complete such a transaction, and believing he was just playing games on the family computer, his parents had happily let him use it for an hour each evening. However, this story highlights other dangers. In the same way that parents of non-disabled children worry about the dangers of their children chatting to strangers online, Aijay's parents became concerned that he, too, could potentially fall victim to those who prey on young and innocent children, perhaps being tricked into revealing personal details about himself or his family or being primed by others to arrange a meeting. The few pounds they paid for the toy were, they considered, nothing to what might have happened had Aijay found his way on to other, less reputable, websites.

Tip! Keep an eye what the child is doing when he is using the computer . . . he may be able to do more than you realize!

ICT and communication

In Chapter 8 we looked at some of the ways technology can be used to help those with communication difficulties. From the relatively simple BIGmack to the more sophisticated communication board, all are essential aids for those who, for whatever reason, need help with their communication.

As well as providing a voice for the child, technology can also be used to encourage sound production. Sound-activated toys and voice-operated software can be used by children who, while not able to use words, can vocalize or make sounds. However, not all communication aids need to be this specialized. A brightly coloured battery-operated parrot that sits on its perch and repeats sounds, words and phrases using the same intonation and accent as the child, or a voice-distorting plastic microphone can motivate even the most reluctant 'speaker'. Similarly, a teddy bear with 'record' and 'play' buttons on each of his footpads can, when programmed with simple commands such as 'Hello, what is your name?' or 'Sing me a song please', encourage both expressive and receptive language skills in a fun and non-threatening way.

While specialist communication aids are generally only available from dedicated suppliers, toys to encourage communication (such as the talking teddy) can often be bought in traditional toyshops or department stores. Those such as the talking parrot and plastic microphone are often found in 'gimmick' stores, both online and on the high street. As with all equipment bought from such stores it is essential that these are thoroughly safety-checked before use to ensure they are able to withstand daily use as well as meeting recommended toy safety standards.

Tip! Always ensure you have a ready supply of new or recharged batteries available. Even the few minutes it takes to locate the battery box, find those that are still fully charged and finally fit them can transform a child who was keen and enthusiastic into one who has become bored with what once was a motivating activity.

ICT across the curriculum

In almost every school across the UK, children study ICT as part of their curriculum. It can help children to acquire new skills, to demonstrate their learning and to participate in activities in a way that no other area of learning can. It is essential, then, that it spans the whole curriculum and that it is not restricted to a timetabled slot once or twice a week.

Technology enhances almost every aspect of our lives. It is present in almost everything we do, whether it is simply carrying a mobile phone in our back pocket, using a digital camera to capture memorable events or going online to research, book and pay for a once-in-a-lifetime holiday. Developments over the past few decades have resulted in a whole range of new and exciting opportunities, not just for us but also for children with severe, profound and multiple learning disabilities. Technology can aid the development of some of the simplest responses and can be accessed, as we have seen, via the smallest of movements such as a blink of the eye or a twitch of the shoulder. It can be used to develop cause and effect, anticipation, cooperation, turntaking, observation, memory and recall and can help increase visual and auditory abilities as well as the development of fine and gross motor skills. Used in more conventional ways, it helps to develop skills across the whole curriculum as well as encouraging online research and the storage and retrieval of data and pictures, albeit at a simple level.

As technology advances, many traditional methods of teaching and learning are being replaced with newer, more exciting alternatives. Interactive whiteboards take the place of conventional chalkboards, laptops replace bulky files and folders and the internet is favoured more and more over conventional methods of research. Increasingly ingenious software encourages awareness and development in all areas of early learning, from the learning of the very earliest skills to the study of the wide range of subjects found within a traditional curriculum, as well personal, social and health education.

Contrary to what some may think, ICT is not just about computers. All children, including those with profound and multiple learning difficulties can make music through movement using specialist equipment such as the Soundbeam®. This device, which uses motion sensors to produce digitally generated sounds is activated by, and responds to, simple movements. It puts the child in control of music making and sound production rather than him having to rely on an adult to help him use, for example, simple percussion instruments. Headphones can allow children with hearing impairments to listen to songs, rhymes and stories without the distraction of background noise, while even those with the most profound hearing loss can use technology to experience music through vibrating chairs or beds. Programmable toys such as Bee-Bot, Roamer or Constructa-Bot (all available from specialist online suppliers) can provide the opportunity for children to practise a wide range of skills including number recognition, sequencing, estimating, concepts such as 'more' and 'less', direction, following instructions, the ability to instruct a programmable toy and, of course, anticipation, turntaking, and cooperation. Simple storybooks with sound buttons, which can be purchased cheaply and easily on the high street, can encourage an interest in reading. Musical mats, dance mats or games consoles with motion-based control, such as the Nintendo Wii®, can motivate even the most able-bodied, but sedentary, child.

> Tip! ICT is not just a subject on the school timetable. It is often used unknowingly in the home as we read to and play with our children.

For many children the use of communication aids and switches can allow them to participate in activities across the whole curriculum as the following stories demonstrate.

Charlie, aged 12, had a severe learning disability and no verbal communication but was able to use a BIGmack by striking it with the side of his fist. This gave him the opportunity to participate fully in a whole range of activities. Before he arrived into school each day, his teacher recorded a simple message, and, as the register was called, he was able to reply 'I'm here today, Mr N' simply by striking the BIGmack. Throughout the day, the message was changed. He was able to 'sing' favourite songs and nursery rhymes along with the rest of his class, and when his teacher paused after the line 'Old MacDonald had a farm' he was able to join in with 'E,I,E,I,O', pre-recorded, of course, on his BIGmack. He could go to the school kitchen and 'ask' to borrow a bowl during cookery sessions, or to the class next door to request the loan of a favourite book at storytime. His new-found independence boosted his confidence and led, in turn, to better and more meaningful learning opportunities.

9-year-old Lucie, a wheelchair user with many uncontrolled and involuntary movements, had recently learned to use a switch. She became very excited by the opportunities this skill allowed her. Motivated by food, she soon became adept at using a switch attached to a food processor to whizz a banana and milk together, making her own milkshake to enjoy each day before she went home. She could participate in pretend play sessions by using her switch to operate a toy washing machine or a drill and toolset and could stop and start the DVD player when watching her favourite DVDs. Her favourite activity, though, was to be 'in charge' of the games during school Christmas or birthday parties. Using a switch to operate the CD player during a game of musical statues, she watched intently as other children danced. She became more animated than usual, though, when, fully aware of her actions, she stopped the music. She laughed and giggled as her friends posed in weird and wonderful positions until she restarted the music and the dancing continued. Unable to control her move-ments, she would never have been able to participate fully in this game but technology had allowed her to be in charge, which, to her, was a real thrill!

The opportunities for every child to use technology to improve learning are endless. These opportunities will, no doubt, continue to increase as tech-nology becomes more advanced and accessible. From the simplest battery-operated toy to the more sophisticated and expensive specialized equipment, no child should be denied access to the skills and learning that technology can provide.

ICT as a motivator

Technology is a great motivator. It can encourage and stimulate otherwise unwilling children to investigate, learn and demonstrate skills that might otherwise have gone unnoticed.

13-year-old Noah was severely autistic. He was reluctant to communicate with those around him despite being able to both sign and speak a few simple words. He showed little interest in people or activities and, like many with autism, pre-ferred his own company to that of other people.

Along with the rest of his class, he participated in a daily hour-long literacy ses-sion. However, unlike the other children Noah sat slumped in his chair for the entire session, showing little interest in any of the activities. This behaviour continued until the day that an interactive white board was installed.

Almost immediately, Noah's attitude changed. He began to show more interest in the stories, words and pre-reading activities on the screen and watched intently as other children took turns at reading and identifying words. His teacher was both pleased and surprised at his sudden interest in reading. She was even more surprised though when, one week later, he suddenly got up from his chair, went to the whiteboard and, carefully pointing to each word in turn, read each one out loud.

Spurred on by this success, his teacher changed the story on the whiteboard and, again, Noah read each word out loud. Over the course of the next few days his teacher introduced new activities to make sure that he was not simply reciting the stories from memory. Noah proved he was able to find words on request, match and read individual words and, even more impressively, could put three words together to form a sentence.

It didn't stop there though. Noah not only started to show more interest in reading but he also began to attempt to write his name. His previously non-existent pencil skills started to develop and, although it took many months, Noah eventually succeeded in writing his first name unaided. With the lack of any written evidence of his skills, his teacher used both a digital camera and a camcorder to record his efforts and a lasting record of his achievements was produced.

In school, ICT is not, of course, restricted to the classroom. The use of switches is particularly effective in a multi-sensory room, especially for those who have profound and multiple learning difficulties. Imagine, for example, lying in a darkened, comfortable and warm environment, surrounded only by scented oils and soft music. Now imagine a floor-to-ceiling bubble tube suddenly bursting into action, glowing gently as a multitude of bubbles rise whenever you reach out and touch a switch that has been placed, conveniently, at your side. The bubbles will attract your attention as they glide towards the ceiling, perhaps changing colours every now and again to maintain your interest. For many children with the most profound learning disabilities this environment can be most motivating of all.

Tip! The immediate feedback technology provides ensures that the time delay between action and reward is minimal, helping to reinforce newly acquired skills and to consolidate and maintain those that have already been achieved.

Finally . . .

Technology is part of all our lives. There is no limit to its uses. In varying forms, it can be used as a motivator, a reward or a means of communication. It can help to develop cognitive, sensory and motor skills, as well as to advance interaction and cooperation, and it promotes successful teaching and learning. It must, and should, be considered an essential part of any curriculum, to be incorporated into each and every day and used at every opportunity.

13 | Assessment, prompts and rewards

Praise the young and they will blossom.

–Irish proverb

There are many aspects to education, all of which affect our teaching in different ways. Some of these, such as the way in which we communicate with a child, how we present or break down tasks or how we handle a child's difficult or challenging behaviour, relate directly to our contact and interaction with him. There are other aspects that will improve our teaching due to an understanding of their importance and relevance. A knowledge of assessment, including how and why we assess, is one of these aspects. Such knowledge is essential across all areas of teaching and learning. It can be used in different ways and for different reasons, and can affect both the child's learning and our own teaching. It can be formal or informal and can be performed either with the child or in isolation from him. It can be used to provide feedback or to determine the next stage in learning as well, of course, as to acknowledge achievements.

This chapter will look at both teacher-based and child-based assessment, as well as exploring some of its uses. The appropriate use of prompting and rewards will also be discussed.

Teacher-based assessment

Assessment is an ongoing process. It serves many purposes and is an essential part of teaching and learning. It can take two main forms, formative and summative. Formative assessment is used on a daily basis in the classroom while summative assessment typically occurs at the end of the school year or on completion of a module or course and can provide grades or levels of achievement as well as qualifications or awards.

Tip! Remember that formative assessment is an assessment **for** learning while summative learning is an assessment **of** learning.

Formative assessment is especially important for those educating children with severe or profound learning disabilities since these children, as we have constantly seen, may not follow usual learning patterns. It allows the teacher to assess learning at any given moment, to continually adapt the teaching style and content and to provide immediate feedback in whatever form is relevant. Changes can also be applied that will aid the child's learning, understanding and motivation, thus ensuring more effective teaching. These changes may be as simple as replacing a standard paintbrush with a stubby paintbrush to help a child with a poor grasp to paint a picture or changing the colour or font size on a computer screen to increase readability. More complex changes can also be identified, such as changing the task or the way of teaching to one more appropriate to the child. As the following story shows, formative assessment can be used across the whole curriculum with children of all ages and abilities.

> *Lucas, aged 9, came into school one morning with a note from his mum describing how, for several weeks, he had struggled to fasten his own shoelaces when getting dressed for school. Keen to help him achieve a little more independence, she asked his teacher for help.*

> *Later that day, as Lucas got dressed after his PE lesson, his teacher watched as he tried to fasten his laces. He was able to complete the first few steps, pulling his laces to tighten the shoe and then crossing them, tucking one end under and pulling tightly again. He successfully made a loop with one end of the lace but was then unable to go any further. His teacher went across to him before frustration set in and he gave up in desperation. 'Lucas' she said, 'let me show you a different way to fasten your laces'. Guiding him both verbally and physically through the task she continued, 'First we need to make two bunny ears . . . then we must take one bunny around the tree . . . and put him into his hole'. Over the next few days Lucas practised tying his shoelaces, always repeating the same instructions (which he referred to simply as his 'bunny story') out loud. His teacher watched on from a distance, helping him as required and continually monitoring and assessing his progress. Within a couple of weeks Lucas was able to fasten his shoelaces without any help from either his teacher or his parents.*

In contrast to formative assessment, which aims to improve learning, summative assessment aims to prove that learning has taken place. It is always positive and provides evidence of progress, focusing on what children can do rather than what they cannot. It can take the form of a written assessment such as an end of year report, a tick list or a certificate to name but a few. While this type of assessment provides evidence of a child's learning and achievements, it does not have any real value in terms of actual learning. Summative assessments can be internal (usually marked by the teacher or other member of staff) or external (marked by people outside of the school or learning environment and who generally have no knowledge of the child).

Evidence of achievements does not always need to be paper-based. Increasingly, photographs and video are used to record children's successes. A 'tick in a box' recording the first step a child takes unaided, perhaps after months of hard work by all involved, does little to record the effort that has gone into it. Photographic or video evidence, however, will not only provide an everlasting record of the moment, but will also record the smile on the child's face as well as the pleasure shown by his teacher or physiotherapist. Copies can also be sent to parents allowing them, too, to share the excitement. A much more meaningful record of a small, but very important, achievement!

> Tip! Video and DVD recordings can be used as means of formative and summative assessment, to both identify learning that may have been missed in a busy classroom and to help plan the way forward.

Child-based assessment

Assessment in the classroom is not just teacher-based and children are increasingly being encouraged to take responsibility for their own learning and reflect upon their achievements. They are encouraged to think through what they have done, either in the short-term or over a period of time, and to consider ways their learning could be improved.

> Tip! Formative assessment can be used to help children, including those with learning disabilities, to be involved in their own assessment.

While many non-disabled children are able to talk about their achievements, perhaps identifying areas where they could have worked harder or achieved more, those with a learning disability will require a different approach. Star charts, rewarding children for continuous progress towards a specific aim, have been used both in the home and in schools for many years. They can also be used, though, as a form of self-assessment. The simple act of sticking their own brightly coloured and well-deserved star onto an easily accessible chart not only serves as a reminder, but also allows children to see how far they are progressing towards their ultimate aim. Figure 13.1 shows an (unfinished) star chart demonstrating progress towards an aim of returning to the classroom after playtime, willingly and unaccompanied, for a whole week.

	Morning	Dinner	Afternoon
Monday	☆	☆	☆
Tuesday	☆	☆	☆
Wednesday	☆	☆	☆
Thursday	☆		
Friday			

My Aim:
I will come back into school by myself everyday

Figure 13.1   A star chart is a tried and tested method of allowing a child to be involved in his own assessment as well as encouraging continued progress towards a specific aim.

Other children may require a different, more immediate, approach.

4-year-old Abbi was a lively little girl with a severe learning disability. Each week, along with the rest of her class, she visited a local nursery where she was encouraged to socialize and play with non-disabled children of her own age. She had many wonderful qualities; she was always smiling, was very loving, and genuinely liked being with other people. However, she was also prone to bouts of aggression and would hit out at other children, especially if they were playing with any of the teddy bears, some of her favourite toys.

Her Statement of Special Educational Needs (see next section) targeted this aggression and she was encouraged to regularly think about her behaviour both in school and at nursery. Her teacher decided to use these visits to help Abbi take control of her own learning and assessment, and her love of teddy bears proved to be an ideal starting point. Just before her class left for nursery, she was reminded of her aim – 'Remember, Abbi, no hitting today' – and given a picture of a teddy bear. She carried this carefully to nursery, where it was pinned to the inside of the classroom door, acting as a visual reminder, a motivator and a potential reward at the same time. Throughout the session her teacher continually praised her for her good behaviour and reminded her, over and over again, of her aim. Finally, if she completed the session without hitting another child, she was allowed to colour the picture just before she left. She then proudly carried it back to school and helped put it, a little tattered and torn, into her file. Later she was able to look back and, with help from her teacher, was able to see that she had fulfilled her aim for the session or, in her words, had been a 'clever girl' at nursery.

Tip! Child-based assessment can take on many forms, but whichever approach is used, it is essential that it always remains both meaningful and relevant to the child.

Why assess?

We have seen above how assessment can help teaching and learning. However, it also serves many other purposes, some of which will be looked at in this section.

A Statement of Special Educational Needs is often one of the first and most important educational assessments for young children with learning disabilities. Commonly referred to simply as a 'Statement', it ensures that they can access the whole range of relevant services essential for their development. It also allows them access to specialist teaching or extra support in either a special or mainstream school should this be required.

The process of obtaining a Statement can be a difficult and time-consuming process as well as one that may be fraught with emotion. (Remember the comment from the mum in Chapter 3?) It begins as parents, teachers or other professionals, concerned about the development of a child, approach their local education authority (LEA) to request a Statutory Assessment. Information is gathered from a range of sources including parents, teachers, educational psychologists, doctors and social services as well as anyone else involved in the education, care and welfare of the child. Once written evidence has been received, the LEA then decides whether or not to proceed with the Statement. Assuming this goes ahead, a six-section document is completed containing information about the child's educational and non-educational requirements as well as the name and type of school most able to meet his needs. It also highlights any additional help required from the local education authority, health service, social services or other agencies to help meet these needs. Monitoring and reviewing arrangements are included to ensure the Statement always remains up to date and relevant. A Statement of Special Educational Needs is usually reviewed at least annually, although this can be more frequent if required. A multidisciplinary team of parents, teachers, therapists and others concerned with the educational, health and social needs of the child, as well as the child himself, all participate in this process.

Most children with a Statement of Special Educational Needs also have an Individual Education Plan, or IEP for short. Targets set within an IEP are different from, and additional to, the educational aims and targets set within a normal differentiated curriculum. Generally, three or four key targets, or strategies, are set at any one time. These can include activities outside as well as inside the classroom, such as sitting quietly during the school assembly, learning to use a spoon at lunchtime or playing with other children in the playground. Targets can be assessed at any time, although ideally an IEP should be reviewed at least twice a year, one of which should be at the child's annual Statement Review. Occasionally, children without a Statement of Special Educational Needs can have their own IEP, especially if they have specific learning difficulties or behavioural problems.

> Tip! Targets set within an IEP should be SMART targets: specific, measurable, achievable, relevant and time related.

Assessment is also vital to enable those in education to determine the skill level of the child and to plan ahead, setting aims that are both relevant and achievable. Whether these aims are to be included in short-term, medium-term or long-term planning, on a lesson-by-lesson, weekly, termly or annual basis, planning cannot take place unless the child has been assessed and a starting point for learning has been identified. Once established, an ongoing cycle of target setting and assessment is then set up enabling the child to learn, develop and progress.

Regular assessment can also help identify children, perhaps with an undiagnosed learning disability, who are failing to progress. For some, this may lead to the identification of a degenerative condition, which may, in turn, lead to greater support for the family. For those already diagnosed with such a condition, regular assessment can monitor the progress of their condition. Assessment also highlights areas in a child's development that may need greater attention, again leading perhaps to a diagnosis or recognition of a particular disability.

Prompts

Prompts are a natural and essential part of learning. We use prompts to guide others through new or difficult tasks, often without thinking, and vary this according to the level of help required. In the same way that Marcus in Chapter 11 learned to complete an alternating sequence of coloured beads using a structured approach and a series of prompts, a well-structured programme of prompting can help all children with severe and profound learning disabilities.

Any programme of prompts will usually start with a physical prompt before progressing onto a gestural prompt and finally a verbal prompt. The amount of prompting given to the child reduces with each stage until the child is able to complete the task unaided. Throughout the whole process, it is important that the teacher talks the child through the task. A child learning to complete a simple shape sorter, for example, may follow this pattern of prompts:

Physical prompt: The teacher works hand-over-hand with the child and, working as one, they complete the shape sorter together.

Gestural prompt: As the child picks up each shape, the teacher points to the relevant hole in the shape sorter, giving the child, in effect, a clue to the next step of the task.

Verbal prompt: The teacher simply talks the child through the task. Perhaps he will be told to 'turn it round', 'look for the round hole' or even 'now put the circle in'.

Not all prompts will be the same and different techniques may be used at each stage according to both the child and the task. The prompts for a different child, learning to pull his own trousers up as part of a dressing programme, may look like this:

Physical Prompt: The child and teacher hold different parts of the trouser waistband and together they pull them up from the ankles to the waist.

Gestural prompt: The teacher mimes pulling up the trousers.

Verbal prompt: The teacher reminds the child to pull his trousers up.

Tip! Don't expect all children to respond to the same prompt. Like everything else prompts will vary according to the each child's needs and abilities.

It is general practice now in almost all schools for teachers to provide evidence of the child's work. Recording the amount of prompting gives a clear indication of how much help has been needed for a child to successfully complete a task. A child completing a worksheet showing his ability to add numbers to ten may well be able to do this unaided. On the other hand, he may have required some level of prompting. The 'good work' sticker, smiley face or gold star may prove to others that he has worked hard to complete the task but it does not indicate how much help has been needed to do so. A simple 'PP' (physical prompt), 'GP' (gestural prompt) or 'VP' (verbal prompt) tucked discreetly into the corner of the page makes this clear without distracting from the child's own work. Had Barney's teacher (Chapter 5) provided this information when he transferred schools his new teacher would have had a much clearer idea of his abilities. The transition would also have been much easier for Barney and the confusion and bewilderment caused by tasks that were too difficult for him could have been avoided.

Rewards

Rewards come in all shapes and sizes and are an essential part of our lives. Whether it is a financial reward for a job well done, the special holiday that took a whole year to save for or a simple hug from a loved one when we achieve our goals, rewards both motivate and inspire us.

Children, too, soon learn the value of rewards. For many, the anticipation of receiving the reward can act as an incentive to succeed. A non-disabled child may work extra hard to achieve good grades in an examination, for example, if he knows he will be rewarded with a new bike, the latest mobile phone or a day out with friends to a nearby theme park. Children with moderate learning disabilities may respond to a star chart, as described earlier, but only if they understand that they must achieve their aim over a period of time before receiving their reward. Children with more severe or profound learning disabilities, however, are less able to make the link between the activity and the reward unless this is given immediately.

Tip! Children who complete their task and then proceed to shout, hit out or destroy work may learn to link the last behaviour with the reward. Now, instead of new behaviours or skills being developed, unwanted ones will simply be reinforced.

A reward can be anything that the child enjoys. This may be a favourite toy or activity, a slice of fruit, a small piece of biscuit or even a few minutes time-out. Even obsessive behaviours can be turned into rewards as the following story shows.

In addition to his autism, Sadiq, aged 8, had a severe developmental delay affecting many areas of his learning. His motivation was poor and he was seldom inclined to do anything simply to please others. Since learning to use scissors when he was 6-years-old he had become obsessed with them and spent endless hours happily cutting paper into tiny, confetti-like pieces. Needless to say, his parents and teachers had learned through experience to keep any scissors, as well as any important paperwork, well out of reach!

However, one day his teacher decided that this obsession might prove useful as a reward. A pair of blunt-ended safety scissors and a piece of paper were placed on his table alongside his work and, through the use of a communication board, his teacher told him 'Work first, Sadiq, then scissors'. It took only a short time for him to understand this and gradually, over time, his teacher was able to introduce two, three and then four pieces of work to be completed before the reward was given. As long as he was able to see the scissors and paper, Sadiq happily completed all his tasks.

Tip! Make sure the reward is of interest to the child and that it is used consistently. It must always be used in the same way if it is to remain successful. The only exception to this rule is the changing interests of the child.

Finally, a word on the use of hugs, cuddles and kisses as a reward. In the same way that we might hug a friend for passing his or her driving test, many children with learning disabilities will also respond to this simple but affectionate type of reward. However, in a world increasingly aware of inappropriate contact between adult and child, rewards such as this are best used only by parents or carers due to their very personal nature.

Finally . . .

This chapter has highlighted the importance of assessment, prompting and use of rewards, three elements of a child's education we do all day and every day, often without realizing. When used in combination, they can have an immense effect on the child's learning as well, as we have seen, on our own teaching.

14 | Classroom essentials

We will either find a way or make one.
−Hannibal, military commander, tactician and strategist (247–182 BC)

Throughout this book we have explored some of the ways children with severe and profound learning disabilities are able to learn. We have discovered, for example, how tasks can be broken down to ensure that learning is successful, how the curriculum can be adapted to suit every child and how surroundings can affect the child's ability to concentrate. We have looked at why some children behave the way they do, how parents can help in their child's education and how the way we speak to children can help their understanding.

As all those in education know, though, it is often the little tricks of the trade that ensure teaching is successful and every teacher will have his or her own tips. This chapter will investigate some of these before moving on to consider the relevance of age-appropriateness.

First, though, the use of simple day boards or books will be investigated as a means of developing anticipation and understanding as well as to help reduce behaviour problems caused by the uncertainty of what lies ahead.

Visual timetables, routine and behaviour

We all need routine. We feel both reassured and comforted when we know what is happening, where we are going, who we will see and even when we will return home. We make notes in diaries and on calendars or set reminders on our mobile phones to make sure we don't forget events and activities that are important to us. Changes to our routine can affect us in different ways. If the change is due to an event we have organized ourselves, such as a holiday or a day out with friends, we can look forward to it with excitement and anticipation. Providing we know about them in advance we can cope with hospital appointments, trips to the dentist or meetings at work, despite the disruption to our usual routine. But if we are faced with an unplanned change or need to rearrange our plans due to, perhaps, a forgotten appointment, this can upset us for the rest of the day. We may make frantic phone calls to reschedule events or dash around, trying to make sure we get everything done, including of course, fitting in that forgotten appointment.

Now, imagine how you would feel if you had a severe or profound learning disability and were unaware of what was happening from one minute to the next. You may have little understanding, if any, of the passage of time. Consequently, you will not know when (or if) you will get your lunch, whether or not you will be going for a swim or even if you will be going home at the end of the day – whenever that might be! Is it any wonder that you may be anxious or irritable or that you may behave in an erratic or unpredictable manner? Visual timetables, also known as visual calendars or dayboards, can help children with learning disabilities to anticipate what lies ahead and to make sense of what otherwise might be a confusing, unpredictable and sometimes frightening world.

> Tip! Providing the child can understand the link between pictures, photographs, symbols, objects or words and what they represent, a visual calendar can provide structure to the day by helping him to physically 'see' the passing of time.

Visual timetables can be adjusted to meet the needs of different children. In their simplest form they may be used to indicate 'now-and-next' activities while others can outline half or even a full day's activities. Some may also use photographs of people or places to provide added information; the child now not only knows what he will be doing but also where and who with. Visual timetables can also be used to indicate changes to the usual timetable with replacement pictures being substituted to reinforce each change. Turning each picture over or removing it completely from the board at the end of each activity indicates to the child that the activity is over and that a change, often a source of confusion in itself, is imminent.

> Tip! Replace pictures or photographs with objects if the child has poor vision or if he relies on touch rather than vision to inform him of what is happening.

In a school setting, visual timetables are often discussed as a group activity first thing each morning, perhaps as part of registration or other early morning activity. Consider, for example, a simplified but typical school day. It may begin, perhaps, with some individual or group work, followed by a drink, swimming, lunch, art and finally another drink before going home. Figure 14.1 shows how this can be recreated using simple line drawings to produce a clear, easily understood visual timetable.

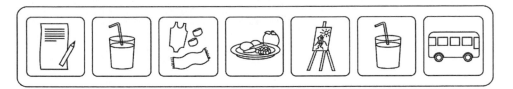

Figure 14.1   A visual timetable of a typical school day.

Some children prefer to carry their timetable in book form so that they can refer to it whenever they wish. 9-year-old Cassie was one of these children.

Cassie had severe learning disabilities and although she had no confirmed diagnosis of autism she displayed many autistic tendencies. She liked to know what was happening at all times and constantly asked her teachers 'What are we doing next . . . and then what after that?'

Along with the rest of her class, she read and discussed the day's events each morning using a large visual timetable displayed on the classroom wall. She returned to it often, touching each picture in turn and talking herself through each activity as it happened. However, she became agitated and restless when she had to leave the classroom, perhaps going to the hall for PE or to the dining room for lunch. Unable to refer to the timetable, her behaviour changed noticeably and her constant questioning increased.

To ease this, she was given her own visual timetable to carry around with her. Pictures, identical to those on the classroom wall were placed into clear plastic pockets within an A5 folder. She carried this continually throughout the day, commenting both on what had happened as well as what was to come. Knowing what was happening, she no longer needed to question those around her and her teachers all commented on how calm she had become.

In the same way that we all may behave in an unpredictable or erratic manner when something unforeseen occurs, children with learning disabilities, not able to understand what is happening, may resort to verbal outbursts, aggression or disruptive behaviours. Visual timetables can help reduce or even eliminate some of these behaviours by reducing fears, concerns and uncertainties about the events and activities of the day ahead.

> Tip! Visual calendars can be used as a means of developing anticipation and understanding as well as to help reduce behaviour problems caused by the uncertainty of what lies ahead.

Making the most of every opportunity

Learning takes place every minute of our waking day. It is not restricted to time, place or subject and those educating children with severe or profound learning disabilities must grasp every opportunity to ensure that learning is a continuous process.

All children learn better when they are given the chance to practice and develop new and existing skills in a range of different contexts and situations. The mathematical skill of counting, as well as an understanding of size and shape, for example, can be practised in a range of settings, not purely as part of a traditional maths lesson.

Riley, aged 10, had severe learning disabilities and a global developmental delay. He worked hard during his lessons, anxious to please his teacher, and glowed with pride when he was rewarded with a smiley face sticker or a verbal 'Clever boy, Riley!'

During his maths lesson he had learned to rote count to ten and was learning to count out objects to six. He was also learning to sort, identify and distinguish between big and little objects. His teacher encouraged him to use these developing skills at every opportunity. At lunchtime he helped set the table by identifying and counting out six big plates for the main course and six little bowls for the pudding. During PE he helped his teacher by giving out six big hoops or six little balls. He was given the task of identifying six big paintbrushes during art lessons and six little toy cars during a geography lesson on transport. The possibilities were endless and, through regular and consistent practise, Riley soon mastered all aspects of the number six including number recognition, counting and counting out as well developing an understanding of big and little.

While the suggestions in the story above may seem obvious, others are less so. Writing a child's name on his picture or painting will help him to recall and identify his own work as well, of course, as helping him to recognize his name. However, if his name is written in the top left-hand corner of his work it can also direct his eye to the starting place on the page, where, once he starts to read, the first word is usually found. Similarly, counting a line of objects from left to right helps develop other pre-reading skills by ensuring that the child's eyes (and possibly his fingers) are moving in the same direction as the words in a sentence.

Tip! Look out for opportunities to practise emerging skills at every opportunity.

Now think back to your own school days. Can you remember when your teachers gave out books or worksheets? Rather than methodically working their way around the whole class, a batch may have been given to the nearest child who would have been told to 'take one and pass it on'. In the mainstream classroom this is often the easiest way to distribute resources. In the special school classroom, though, it is often quicker for the teacher to do it herself. But think of all those missed opportunities for learning. Taking turns, sharing, interaction, anticipation, eye-contact, communication and fine and gross motor skills, as well, of course, the ability to take just one item are just some of the skills that can be practised and refined. An alternative way of doing this is, of course, to give these resources to one child and allow him to give them out. This not only provides him with the opportunity to practise many of the skills listed above but also to develop those in one-to-one correspondence, a basic requirement of any numeracy curriculum.

Children with the most profound and multiple learning difficulties can also benefit from a cross-curricular approach. A child opening his mouth as a spoonful of food is lifted from his bowl is showing signs of anticipation, remembering that this action is the forerunner of being fed. However, anticipation can be developed in many other ways. Take, for example, the well-loved traditional rhyme 'Round and round the garden'.

5-year-old Alissa had profound and multiple learning difficulties. She enjoyed being with her favourite people and smiled in recognition when she saw them. She loved being tickled and would chuckle loudly at the slightest touch. For her,

'Round and round the garden' was an ideal way of further developing her antici-
pation skills.

Sitting opposite her, her teacher started the rhyme, using her finger to draw
circles on Alissa's hand as she did so. 'Round and round the garden, like a
teddy bear, one step . . . two steps . . . ' Pausing briefly after each 'step' up
Alissa's arm, she began to build excitement and anticipation. The biggest
pause, though, was reserved for the last line'. And a . . . ' Sitting with hands
ready to pounce and eyes and mouth wide open her teacher waited for Alissa
to react. Knowing what was coming next, Alissa began to laugh, squirming
in her chair as she did so. Only then did her teacher finish the rhyme ' . . .
tickly under there!', accompanied , of course by that big tickle she was
anticipating!

The stories of Riley and Alissa show how cross-curricular teaching can be
used to make the most of every opportunity. No longer in isolation, their new
and developing skills can be practised to perfection to be used in meaningful,
everyday situations. After all, isn't this what teaching is all about?

It's all in the presentation

The way we present tasks can make a big difference to learning. Whether this
presentation relates to one task or a series of them, it is important to consider
the impact of presentation upon the child's ability to succeed.

10-year-old Sebastian had a moderate to severe learning disability and, while
keen to work and eager to please, could not resist touching or fiddling with any-
thing put in front of him.

Each morning, on arrival into school, he was given three tasks to complete before
the end of the session. Unfortunately, his excitement and eagerness resulted in
puzzle pieces being mixed with counters, threading beads being wrapped up in
worksheets and crayons being posted into his shape sorter.

His teacher was desperate. Keen to help him develop organizational skills she
eventually devised a system that she simply referred to as his 'in and out trays'.
She placed two differently coloured plastic trays on his table, a green one in the
top left corner and a yellow one in the top right corner. Each morning she care-
fully placed his work into the green tray. (This, remember, is the starting point
for reading.) Over time she encouraged him to remove one task at a time, com-
plete it, then put it into the yellow tray. Now instead of just having three pieces
of work randomly positioned in front of him, he had an organized system of
working and everyone was happy.

The way in which Sebastian's work was presented helped him to work methodically through a series of tasks. Presentation is also important, however, for individual tasks. Even a simple activity like counting can be affected by the way in which it is presented.

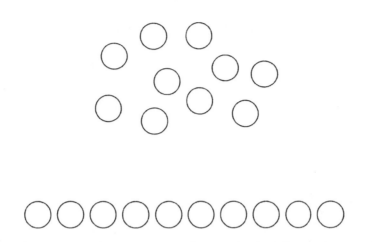

Figure 14.2 Different ways of presenting the task can make the difference between failure and success.

Figure 14.2 shows how two different ways of presenting the same task can help a child succeed. In the first example, ten counters have been simply dropped at random on to the table. There is no structure to the group and, as a result, they are difficult to count. The second example, however, shows them presented in a straight line where, clearly laid out, they can be counted systematically from left to right increasing the child's chance of success. Only after he is confident counting those presented in this way can he be taught strategies and techniques to help him count those scattered randomly in front of him.

Presentation applies, too, to something as simple as our writing style. While almost all adults in the UK can write, we all do it differently. Even those who were taught at the same time, in the same place and by the same person develop their own unique style of writing. Despite this variation each one of us is adept at reading many different writing styles. We know that letters or words written differently will still read the same. An *f* with or without a tail is still, after all, an *f*, or a word written in capital letters is still the same word when written in lower case letters, despite its very different appearance. Children with learning disabilities may however, struggle to understand this concept. Consider the writing styles in Figure 14.3.

fried eggs for my breakfast

fried eggs for my breakfast

fried eggs for my breakfast

fried eggs for my breakfast

fried eggs for my breakfast

fried eggs for my breakfast

Figure 14.3 Different writing styles affect the way words appear when written. This, in turn, may affect how they are perceived and read.

Notice how some of the letters differ and how the overall appearance of the sentences changes according to the font. These different fonts are only a few of those available on many home computers; imagine how much more variation there will be when individual handwriting styles are added to this mix.

While we have no control over the types of fonts used in reading books, on preprinted worksheets or on signs in the community, we can help minimize any confusion by ensuring that in the classroom, at least, we try to maintain some continuity. Making sure that everyone follows the same guidelines, perhaps using **t** instead of **t** or **f** instead of *f* can help avoid confusion caused by their different appearances and maybe go some way towards helping a child learn to read.

> Tip! Agree on a handwriting style and make sure everybody uses it.

As the story below shows, though, while consistency is important for those with learning disabilities, there are times when consistency of presentation is not always appropriate.

12-year-old Leila was learning to recognize numbers. Her teacher was thrilled as she told everyone that, after only two weeks, Leila could already identify the number 5 without any help.

One day, though, a different teacher came into the class to help assess Leila. She placed five cards, at random, on the table, each one displaying a different number, and asked Leila to find the number 5. Leila looked confused and reached out for the card nearest her right hand, only to be told to try again. After several attempts, the new teacher decided that the task was beyond Leila's capabilities.

The following day the two teachers discussed Leila's performance from the previous day. It was then that they realized the problem. In order to maintain consistency, her teacher had always presented the numbers in sequence on Leila's table. As each new number was introduced she simply placed it, in sequence, on the end of the line. However, instead of learning to recognize the new number Leila had simply learned to select the card at the end – and in doing so, she always got it correct!

Leila's teacher had followed the guidelines of presentation with care and precision. As this story shows, though, it is important for those working with learning disabled children to know when to vary the rules on presentation to ensure that successful learning really can take place.

> Tip! Remember that all rules, on occasion, can be broken. The skill lies in knowing when to stick to them and when not to!

Interpreting responses

We all like to think that we are skilled at interpreting the responses and behaviours of others. We know the meaning of facial expressions such as a smile, a frown or a look of boredom. There are times, though when responses and behaviours are not all they seem.

This was demonstrated one day when a medical student, visiting a special school for the first time, joined a group of 5- to 7-year-olds for storytime. She was shocked to see a child recoil in horror as the teacher reached the part in a familiar story where a dragon 'attacked' one of the children. Mentioning this later, she discovered that instead of being afraid of this part of the story, the boy, knowing what was about to happen, was wriggling on his chair in anticipation of a tickle from the teacher (the 'attack'). Unfortunately for him another child got the tickle that day, but that didn't stop him showing what, to an unfamiliar onlooker, appeared to be signs of horror and dread.

> Tip! Knowing the child can allow you to accurately interpret his behaviours, responses and reactions.

Some behaviours, unlike those demonstrated by the boy in the story above, are displayed unintentionally. This is particularly noticeable in children who suffer from certain forms of epilepsy.

Miss R started her new job as a teaching assistant in a class of eight children all of whom had severe or profound learning disabilities. She soon got to know each child's capabilities and became a valued and well-trusted member of the class team.

She had a particular interest in Otto, a 6-year-old boy with profound and multiple learning difficulties who, she said, reminded her of her younger brother. One day, after a busy session working with Otto, she reported back to the teacher. 'Otto has worked really hard today' she said. 'He keeps turning his head towards me and laughing. He is such a happy boy and I'm sure he knows me already.' The class teacher stopped for a moment before explaining that, while Otto may have enjoyed his work, the behaviours Miss R was describing were, in fact, a type of epileptic seizure.

Miss R was surprised to find that seizures could present in this way. Like many people, she held the common belief that seizures only took the form of shaking, jerking, falling to the floor, dribbling and loss of consciousness. Had she known about Otto's particular type of epilepsy she would have been better placed to interpret his actions correctly and look for other, more accurate signs of recognition, enjoyment and pleasure.

> Tip! Epileptic seizures take on many different forms. Be aware of how they affect the child you are working with.

Do unto others . . .

It is often difficult to imagine what other people are thinking or feeling. We can try to talk through thoughts and feelings, especially with friends or relatives, but if that other person is a child with a learning disability this becomes more difficult. We can attempt to read their thoughts by interpreting their facial expressions, actions and vocalizations, but we cannot be sure we are always interpreting them correctly. We can try and guess, too, the reasons for some of their actions and reactions, but again, we have no way of ensuring we will be right. We may have more success, though, if we have experienced some of the activities we automatically expect them to enjoy.

Mr T was the grandfather of 6-year-old Connor, a sociable boy with Down's Syndrome and a big, happy personality. Mr T regularly came into school to help out, especially enjoying Friday afternoon structured play sessions. He would happily play in the sand with a group of children, join them in the Wendy House or help clean them up after a messy painting session. But he refused to have anything to do with the trays of cold, slimy jelly used to develop tactile and fine motor skills. Unable to understand his reaction to the jelly, the other adults in the group smiled at his facial expressions as he watched children playing happily with it, unable to believe they were actually enjoying it!

Until, that is, the day a new child started in the class. One Friday afternoon, along with the rest of the class, she took her turn in the jelly, and just like Mr T, she hated it. She cried, pulled her hands out and stubbornly refused to have any-thing to do with it. She was given, instead, trays filled with bubbly water, uncooked pasta, large brightly coloured semi-transparent beads and even shred-ded paper, all of which she tolerated and some of which she enjoyed.

At this point Mr T approached the teacher. 'I can tell you why she doesn't like it' he said. He described how the cold, slimy feel of the jelly made his skin creep and how, in some strange way, he could only describe it as 'eerie'.

The newly qualified teacher in Connor's class was surprised by the reaction of both Mr T and the little girl. Her limited experience had led her to believe that all children enjoyed jelly-play and she had no reason to believe otherwise.

Many years before this situation arose, a different teacher in another school always made sure her staff experienced for themselves the activities that were given to the children. When foot spas were first introduced to the school, each member of the staff spent a relaxing 15 minutes using them before discussing and comparing their feelings. Everyone had a different view and while most found them calming and restful a few found them noisy, ticklish and irritating. By experiencing activities such as this for themselves they began to appreciate that everyone had different views and opinions and consequently their under-standing and tolerance levels were increased.

Tip! Always try out activities and experiences for yourself before giving them to the children you are working with.

To act or not to act . . .

It is a well known fact that most teachers have, to some extent, a little bit of the actor in them. This is not to say that teaching is the domain only of those who are natural extroverts. Many teachers (including teaching assistants and support staff) are quiet and reserved outside of the classroom, but once in front of a group of children, their bubbly outgoing side takes command. Their ability to stand up with confidence, bringing lessons to life by injecting them with fun and humour, will help ensure that they, and their lessons, will be remembered long after school days are over. On the other hand, shy, retiring and self-conscious educators who struggle to hold the attention and subsequent control of the children they are teaching are soon forgotten.

We all remember favourite teachers from our own school days. More than likely they would be the ones who fell into the first of the two categories above. No doubt they may have indulged in a little overacting. Almost certainly they would have been unafraid to appear a little foolish in a bid to enhance their teaching. They would also have been experts at interaction, knowing how to get the most out of each and every child. Those teaching children with severe and profound learning disabilities need to follow the example of these exceptional teachers. The ability to, perhaps, switch between different voices, exaggerate facial expressions and body movements and involve the child in the lesson will help to both gain and maintain the attention of the children they are teaching as well as to motivate and inspire them.

The ability to mingle acting with teaching, however, can only be matched by the ability to know when not to use it. A class full of excited, overactive or fidgety children will only become more excited, overactive or fidgety if the teacher continues to overact. In these circumstances, a calm, relaxed and soothing approach is needed. No longer the actor, clown, comedian, musician or all-round entertainer, the teacher must now become a pacifier and peacemaker and the ability to switch between these two roles must always remain an essential part of teaching.

One final point: it is reassuring for many to learn that young children and those with learning disabilities do not judge others in the same way that adults do. It really doesn't matter that the funny face you pull is not your most flattering look nor whether that deep, gruff growl you try to make sounds nothing like the bear in the book you are reading. Nor does it matter that you can't sing in tune or that your enthusiastic actions are just a little bit too dramatic. The fact that you are willing and able to use your natural 'talents' to put on an act for the benefit of your teaching is more important than whether or not your stage skills are perfect.

> Tip! Don't be afraid to make a fool of yourself at times. It will enhance your teaching and make learning more fun.

Age appropriateness

The question of age appropriateness will apply, at some point, to many things that children and young people with learning disabilities do. It may be the clothes they wear, the activities they do, the songs they sing or the television programmes they watch.

A 4-year-old child playing happily in a sand tray is a commonplace sight in homes and schools throughout the UK. This simple activity promotes the development of many skills and concepts and is actively encouraged as a fun and exciting part of learning. However, give a learning disabled 17-year-old the same activity and somehow, even if his intellectual age is similar to that of the 4-year-old, the activity may be deemed inappropriate. Similarly, a brightly coloured rattle hanging from a toddler's pushchair is considered acceptable while a similar toy suspended from the wheelchair of a 14-year-old with severe or profound learning disabilities may be scowled upon. Occasionally, it may be possible to substitute other activities or equipment in a bid to make them more suitable for the older child. Replacing sand with flour when encouraging tactile exploration or fine motor skills, for example, or changing the rattle for maracas may be one way around this perceived problem. However, it must be remembered that not all substitutes are as effective as the original; flour has very different tactile qualities to sand and the maracas may not have the same visual appeal as the brightly coloured rattle.

Age appropriateness is not restricted to children and young people. It can apply in just the same way to fully grown adults. A non-disabled adult man wearing a Mickey Mouse tie to a party, for example, may be considered to be an individual dresser, a little wacky, or a bit of an extrovert. However, allow a learning disabled man of the same age to wear a similar tie and the attitude of those around him may be very different. Disapproving comments such as 'Wouldn't you think they would dress him for his age?' or 'He's 35 but they still treat him as child' are, unfortunately, all too common. Unlike the previous examples, the choice of tie has nothing to do with developmental age, yet while it is acceptable for the non-disabled wearer to show his individuality the man with a learning disability is frowned upon.

Different people will all have very different views on age appropriateness. Some will endeavour to ensure that all resources and activities are suitable for the child's chronological age while others will be more concerned that they are relevant for his level of development. However, if you are one of those who fall into the first group it may be worth asking yourself this simple question before you struggle to find age appropriate alternatives: 'Is age appropriateness the child's problem . . . or is it mine?'

Finally . . .

In the same way that children with severe, profound or multiple learning disabilities are all unique, those teaching, supporting or living with them must develop their own distinctive ways of working. What works for one person will not necessarily work for another so be adventurous and if the approach you are using doesn't work, try a different one. Use your imagination as well as your expertise and, over time it will become second nature to adapt your teaching to suit the needs of the children in your care.

Hopefully some of the tips, techniques and suggestions outlined in this chapter, as well as throughout the book as a whole, will help you develop awareness of ways in which children with learning disabilities learn, achieve and succeed. Keep your mind open to new ideas and as you teach you will continue to learn. Share ideas, thoughts and feelings with those around you and never give in.

Whatever you decide to do now, whether you put your newly acquired knowledge into practise or delve further into any of the areas covered, go ahead and do it with confidence. Take pride in your abilities, aim high, enjoy your successes and never underestimate what you are able to achieve.

Further reading

Medical conditions and syndromes

Autism and Early Years Practice. 2nd ed., Kate Wall. Sage Publications Ltd, 2009.

Autism: A Parent's Guide. Hilary Hawkes. Need2Know, 2009.

Down's Syndrome: The Essential Guide. Antonia Chitty and Victoria Dawson. Need2Know, 2010.

Down Syndrome (The Facts). 3rd ed., Mark Selikowitz. Oxford University Press, 2008.

Medical Conditions: A Guide for the Early Years. Pam Dewis. Continuum, 2007.

A Practical Guide to Autism: What Every Parent, Family Member and Teacher Needs to Know. Fred R. Volkmar and Lisa A. Wiesner. John Wiley & Sons, 2009.

Learning disabilities – general

An A to Z Practical Guide to Learning Difficulties. Harry Ayers and Francesca Gray. David Fulton Publishers, 2006.

Profound and multiple learning difficulties / multi-sensory impairment / deafblind

Deaf-blind Infants and Children: A Developmental Guide. J. M. McInnes and J. A. Treffry. University of Toronto Press, 1993.

Profound and Multiple Learning Difficulties. Corinna Cartwright and Sarah Wind-Cowie. Continuum, 2005.

Supporting Children with Multiple Disabilities. 2nd ed., Michael Mednick. Continuum, 2007.

Communication

Access to Communication: Developing the Basics of Communication for People Who Have Severe Learning Disabilities Through Intensive Interaction. 2nd ed., Melanie Nind, and Dave Hewitt. David Fulton Publishers, 2006.

Objects of Reference: Promoting Early Symbolic Communication. 3rd ed., Adam Ockelford. Royal National Institute for the Blind, 2002.

The PECS Training Manual. 2nd ed. Lori Frost and Andy Bondy. Pyramid Educational Products Inc., 2002.

Teaching Communication Skills to Students with Severe Disabilities. 2nd ed., June E. Downing. Brookes Publishing Co., 2005.

Challenging behaviour / ADHD

ADHD. Finton O'Regan. Continuum, 2007.

Turning the Tables on Challenging Behaviour: A Practitioner's Perspective to Transforming Challenging Behaviours in Children, Young People and Adults with SLD, PMLD or ASD. Peter Imray. David Fulton Publishers, 2007.

Curriculum, teaching and assessment

500 Tips for Working with Special Needs. Sally Brown, Sally Harwood, Betty Vahid. Routledge, 1998

A Sensory Approach to Teaching the Curriculum: For Pupils with Profound and Multiple Learning Difficulties. Judy Davis. David Fulton Publishers, 2001.

A Sensory Curriculum for Very Special People: A Practical Approach to Curriculum Planning. Flo Longhorn. Souvenir Press Ltd, 1988.

Special Needs and the Beginning Teacher. Peter Benton and Tim O'Brien. Continuum, 2001

Surviving and Succeeding in SEN. Fintan O'Regan. Continuum, 2007.

Targeting Assessment in the Primary Classroom: Strategies for Planning, Assessment, Pupil Feedback and Target Setting. Shirley Clarke. Hodder Education, 1998.

Family

Grandparenting a Child with Special Needs. Charlotte E. Thompson. Jessica Kingsley Publishers, 2009.

My Brother is Different: A Book for Young Children Who Have a Brother or Sister with Autism. Louise Gorrod. National Autistic Society, 2003.

Useful websites

The websites listed below are only a few of the very many that can be found online. They have been grouped into categories for ease of use, although many will have information that crosses the categories.

While all sites have been checked prior to inclusion, no responsibility can be held for the content and information offered by any of the websites listed.

Medical conditions and syndromes

Angelman Syndrome Support Education & Research Trust (Assert) – www.angelmanuk.org
Association for Spina Bifida & Hydrocephalus (ASBAH) – www.asbah.org
Cerebra – www.cerebra.org.uk
Cri-Du-Chat Syndrome – www.criduchat.co.uk
Down's Syndrome Association – www.downs-syndrome.org.uk
Epilepsy Action – www.epilepsy.org.uk
Fragile X – www.fragilex.org.uk
Meningitis Research Foundation – www.meningitis.org
National Autistic Society (NAS) – www.autism.org.uk
National Society for Epilepsy – www.epilepsysociety.org.uk
Newlife Foundation for Disabled Children – www.bdfnewlife.co.uk
Prader Willi Syndrome – www.pwsa.co.uk
Retts Syndrome – www.rettsyndrome.org.uk
SCOPE – www.scope.org.uk

Learning disabilities – general

About Learning Disabilities – www.aboutlearningdisabilities.co.uk
The British Institute of Learning Disabilities (BILD) – www.bild.org.uk
Bibic – www.bibic.org.uk
Department for Children, Schools and Families – www.dcsf.gov.uk
Foundation for People with Learning Disabilities – www.learningdisabilities.org.uk
Intellectual Disability and Health Information – www.intellectualdisability.info
Mencap – www.mencap.org.uk

National Health Service (NHS) – www.nhs.uk
Office for Advice, Assistance, Support and Information on Special Needs
  (OAASIS) – www.oaasis.co.uk
UK Learning Disabilities Website – www.ukld.ukcharity.com

Sensory impairments

Deafblind UK – www.deafblind.org.uk
Royal National Institutes of Blind People (RNIB) – www.rnib.org.uk
Royal National Institute for Deaf People (RNID) – www.rnid.org.uk
SENSE – www.sense.org.uk

Communication

Ace Centre – www.ace-centre.org.uk
Afasic – www.afasic.org.uk
Communication Matters – www.communicationmatters.org.uk
Intensive Interaction – www.intensiveinteraction.co.uk
Makaton – www.makaton.org
Picture Exchange Communication System (PECS) – www.pecs.com
Total Communication – www.totalcommunication.org.uk

Behaviour, attention and hyperactivity

The Challenging Behaviour Foundation – www.thecbf.org.uk
Hyperactive Children's Support Group – www.hacsg.org.uk
The National Attention Deficit Disorder Information and Support Service
  (ADDISS) – www.addiss.co.uk

Mainly for teachers

Classroom Assistant – www.classroom-assistant.net
Down Syndrome Educational Trust (DownsEd) – www.downsed.org
EQUALS – www.equals.co.uk
NASEN – www.nasen.org.uk
SEN Teacher – www.senteacher.org
TeacherNet – www.teachernet.gov.uk
Teachers' TV – www.teachers.tv
TES Connect – www.tes.co.uk

Mainly for families

Antenatal Results and Choices (ARC) – www.arc-uk.org
BLISS – www.bliss.org.uk

The Child Bereavement Charity – www.childbereavement.org.uk
Child Death Helpline – www.childdeathhelpline.org.uk
Children Today – www.childrentoday.org.uk
Compassionate Friends– www.tcf.org.uk
Contact a Family – www.cafamily.org.uk
Directgov – www.parentcentre.gov.uk
Disabilities Trust – www.disabilities-trust.org.uk
First-tier Tribunal (Special Educational Needs and Disability) – www.sendist.
  gov.uk
Independent Panel for Special Education Advice (IPSEA) – www.ipsea.org.
  uk
MedicAlert – www.medicalert.org.uk
Round Table Children's Wish (RTCW) – www.rtcw.org
Sibs – www.sibs.org.uk
Special Kids in the UK – www.specialkidsintheuk.org
Special Needs Kids – www.special-needs-kids.co.uk

Sensory toys and equipment

Rompa – www.rompa.com
The Sensory Company – www.thesensorycompany.co.uk
SpaceKraft – www.spacecraft.co.uk
Tfh – www.specialneedstoys.com
Total Sensory – www.totalsensory.co.uk

Information technology

Ability Net – www.abilitynet.org.uk
HelpKidzLearn – www.helpkidzlearn.com
Inclusive Technology – www.inclusive.co.uk
Keytools Ltd – www.keytools.co.uk
National Centre for Technology in Education – www.ncte.ie
QED (Quality Enabling Devices) – www.QEDonline.co.uk
Semerc – www.semerc.com
SENsation CTS Ltd – www.sen-sation.co.uk
Soundbeam – www.soundbeam.co.uk

Glossary

ABC recording – a method of recording the antecedent, behaviour and consequences of challenging behaviours.

Age appropriateness – the relevance of activities, situations and events to a person's chronological age rather than to developmental age.

Assessment, formative – an informal assessment to improve learning.

Assessment, summative – a formal assessment that proves learning has taken place.

Attention Deficit Hyperactivity Disorder (ADHD) – a condition in which the child displays excessive activity, disruptive behaviours and poor focusing and attention skills.

Attention span – the length of time a person can attend to a task without being distracted or losing concentration.

Augmentative and Alternative Communication – forms of communication that supplement or support speech and writing.

Backward chaining – a way of breaking down tasks and teaching the steps in the reverse order.

BIGmack/LITTLEmack – simple battery-operated communication aids that have the facility to record, delete and re-record short messages appropriate to the child's needs.

Cause and effect – an understanding that an action can make something happen.

Challenging behaviour – behaviour that can put the child or others around him at risk due to its intensity, frequency or duration.

Cognitive ability – the ability to use knowledge acquired through thought, experience and understanding as well through the senses.

Concentration span – the length of time a person can concentrate on a task or activity, usually to the exclusion of everything else, before interest is lost or thoughts wander elsewhere.

Concept keyboard/overlay keyboard – a flat board with a programmable grid over which a sheet with pictures or symbols can be placed and which can be used as a simplified keyboard.

Cross-curricular – an approach to teaching and learning that spans and links all subjects of the curriculum.

Deafblind – a condition in which there is impairment, of varying degrees, to both vision and hearing.

Degenerative condition – a condition in which there is a progressive loss of skills and abilities.

Differentiation – the adjustment of teaching to ensure the lesson or activity meets the different learning needs of every child.

Echolalia – the repetition or echoing of words or phrases spoken by another person, often using the same tone of voice and intonation.

Eye-pointing – using the eyes to point to favoured objects, people or activities.

Fine motor skills – skills involving the small muscles of the body, especially in the hands and fingers.

Forward chaining – a way of breaking down tasks and teaching the steps in the correct sequential order.

Generalization – the ability to transfer a skill from one activity to another similar activity.

Gestural prompt – a prompt using gestures such as pointing or nodding.

Global developmental delay – a uniform delay in the development of most, or all, areas of development.

Gross motor skills – skills involving the large muscles of the body such as arms, legs and trunk.

Hand-over-hand – a way of working in which the adult's hand covers the child's hand to support him through a task or action.

Incidental learning – unplanned or untaught learning.

Individual Education Plan (IEP) – a legal document that helps in the planning, teaching and reviewing of a child's progress.

Information (and) Communication Technology (ICT) – the use of computers or any other electronic equipment or communication device to store, retrieve and send information.

Intellectual ability – the ability to reason and understand.

Intelligence Quotient (IQ) – an assessment and measurement of intelligence.

Key words – the main information-carrying words in a sentence.

Language, expressive – the use of speech, sign, symbols, writing, and other forms of communication to express feelings and make needs known.

Language, receptive – the comprehension of speech, sign, symbols, writing, and other forms of communication.

Learning difficulty/specific learning difficulty – a difficulty in one or more areas of learning which, with correct support and teaching, have the potential to be resolved.

Learning disability – a life-long intellectual impairment affecting the ability to learn and progress at the same rate as others of the same age.

Makaton – a method of communication using sign, speech and symbols.

Multi-sensory – referring to more than two of the senses.

Multi-sensory room (also known as sensory room, white room or Snoezelen) – a calming, relaxing or stimulating environment designed to stimulate the senses though the use of specialized lighting, soothing sounds, tactile surfaces and subtle fragrances.

Object of reference – an object used to aid communication and which represents an activity, person or event.

Object permanence – the understanding that an object can exist even when it is out of sight.

One-to-one correspondence – matching one object to one other, for example, giving one pencil to every child or putting one spoon in every bowl.

Orthotic boots – specialist boots offering extra ankle or arch support and which help to provide foot support for walking and standing. Commonly known as Piedro boots.

Passive learning – see incidental learning.

Physical prompt – a prompt in which the learner is fully assisted to complete a task, perhaps by hand-over-hand or other methods.

Picture Exchange Communication System (PECS) – a system of communication in which begins with pictures being exchanged for objects or activities and continues to develop discrimination, abstract concepts and simple sentences.

Profound and multiple learning difficulties (PMLD) – a combination of a profound learning disability as well as any combination of sensory and/or physical disabilities and complex health and medical conditions.

Rise and fall table – a height-adjustable table, especially useful for wheelchair users, which can easily be adjusted to meet individual requirements.

Rote counting – reciting numbers in sequence, usually from memory.

Sensory curriculum – a curriculum that makes use of and develops all of the senses.

Simi-specs – spectacles designed to simulate different visual impairments.

Statement of Special Educational Needs – a legal document setting out a child's needs and detailing any extra help required to achieve these.

Statutory Assessment – a detailed assessment of a child's educational and other needs and one of the first steps towards a Statement of Special Educational Needs. A statutory assessment does not always lead to a Statement being issued.

Tactile defensiveness – sensitivity to touch often resulting in refusal or avoidance of touch. Individual children may be tactile defensive to different textures.

Terrible twos – a development stage, usually occurring around the age of 2 years when children develop temper tantrums and negative behaviours as they begin to become more assertive and independent.

Total Communication – a system of communication using a range of different types of communication, depending upon the child's individual requirements.

Verbal prompt – a spoken prompt.

Visual timetable – a timetable using pictures, photographs, symbols, objects or words to help provide structure to the day and enable children to understand and anticipate what is happening.

Index